Illicit Financial Flows

THE ECONOMY OF ILLICIT TRADE IN WEST AFRICA

OECD
BETTER POLICIES FOR BETTER LIVES

Please cite this publication as:
OECD (2018), *Illicit Financial Flows: The Economy of Illicit Trade in West Africa*, OECD Publishing, Paris.
http://dx.doi.org/10.1787/9789264268418-en

ISBN 978-92-64-24520-4 (print)
ISBN 978-92-64-26841-8 (PDF)

Photo credits: Cover © AFP PHOTO/JESUS ALCAZAR, © REUTERS/Akintunde Akinleye

Corrigenda to OECD publications may be found on line at: *www.oecd.org/about/publishing/corrigenda.htm*.

Foreword

People often say that criminal activity is like a balloon: if you squeeze at one end, the air will shift and pop up somewhere else. Similarly, you can try to crack down on smugglers – for example, by restricting their use of land routes – only to find they are using sea routes instead. This is why targeted interventions often have limited impact on criminal activity: they need to look at the big picture, to tell the whole story of how the air moves in the balloon.

This report tells the story of people with few livelihood options. It is a complex story, with many interconnections; at the heart of which is globalisation. While globalisation has spread a plethora of beneficial innovations around the world, it has also had many negative consequences in both rich and poor countries: in fact, security problems in the advanced nations are closely related to the development challenges faced by the rest of the world. Yet the side effects of globalisation are particularly strong in the world's poorest countries – those least equipped to respond to these impacts.

This report looks beyond specific countries to capture illicit financial flows (IFFs) in the West African region. It zeroes in on illicit trade to illustrate the larger picture: criminal activity as a source of IFFs, its relationship to development and the challenges it poses for governance. This nexus has received little attention, yet criminal activity has a significant negative impact on development.

Why focus on West Africa? Several countries in the region post extremely low development indicators, have weak state institutions and present capacity gaps for regulation. As in many developing countries, a large share of economic activity takes place in the informal economy. Not everything informal is bad: in fact, the informal sector often provides precious livelihoods, particularly for the poor. Yet what happens informally happens outside the checks and balances of regulatory systems. As a result, illicit or criminal activities may flourish more easily, with negative implications for governance, peace, stability and development. Under these conditions, resource diversion and illegal acts affecting a country's development can thrive, damage the integrity of institutions, and distort political governance in ways that disrupt the relationship between citizens and the state. Across the region, IFFs are known to have resourced violent and protracted conflicts; in the Sahel, they resource terrorist groups. Although it is impossible to isolate specific conditions leading directly to criminal activity, structural factors (such as high unemployment and income inequality, exposure to violence, low levels of gross domestic product and weak institutional capacities) are known to contribute to a country's vulnerability.

This report feeds into a strategy of the OECD Development Co-operation Directorate to increase data and evidence in the area of IFFs to help address the risks they pose to development. This strategy started with the publication of *Illicit Financial Flows from Development Countries: Measuring OECD Responses*. Two other publications followed, *Few and Far: The Hard Facts on Asset Recovery*, and *Tracking Anti-Corruption and*

Asset Recovery Commitments, tracing the efforts of OECD member countries to increase the investigation and repatriation of stolen assets to their countries of origin.

This new report, *Illicit Financial Flows: The Economy of Illicit Trade in West Africa*, builds on the first three in the series, focusing on West Africa. It is founded on extensive background research, which a large group of experts (acknowledged in a separate section) helped deliver. Institutional partners from the region – the African Development Bank, the Intergovernmental Action Group on Money Laundering in West Africa and the New Partnership for Africa's Development – provided access to local knowledge and networks, helping to understand the issues in their context. The World Bank contributed unique expertise and knowledge on the financing of terrorism. A Reference Group helped tap into an extensive regional and international network of experts and practitioners, who contributed either as peer reviewers or key informants. To complement the research, the Reference Group helped select case studies illustrating the dynamics of illicit activities in the region.

Beyond a vast review of literature, this report also draws on extensive interviews in the region and elsewhere, as well as on a technology-enabled survey (using mobile phone services in some West African countries) and focus-group interviews with migrants landing in Europe, all to gather diverse perspectives. Contributors include West African law-enforcement officials and development practitioners, as well as decision makers and citizens. To ensure their safety, we do not name these sources here, but their contributions are at the heart of the report.

Illicit Financial Flows: The Economy of Illicit Trade in West Africa calls for a comprehensive view of the linkages between development, governance and globalisation's dark side. We hope it will contribute to a new way of thinking about these interconnections.

The report also contributes to a new way of understanding IFFs, as reflected in the 2030 Agenda for Sustainable Development which acknowledges IFFs as inherently linked to development. The overarching message is timeless: resolving *some* of the world's most pressing problems, in this instance IFFs, requires responding to development challenges, and working in countries at all levels of development to address each part of the spectrum – source, transit and destination. Tackling global challenges requires reforms to happen on all sides.

Phil Mason
Co-chair of the Anti-Corruption Task Team
Senior Anti-Corruption Adviser
UK Department for International Development

Jorge Moreira da Silva
Director
Development Co-operation Directorate
Organisation for Economic Co-operation and Development

Acknowledgements

The OECD has published this study in partnership with the African Development Bank (AfDB), the Inter-Governmental Action Group against Money Laundering in West Africa (GIABA), the New Partnership for Africa's Development (NEPAD Agency) and the World Bank.

The production of this report was initiated by Alan Whaites and Alessandra Fontana, and drawn to a conclusion by Nadine Gbossa, Catherine Anderson, Luca Maiotti and Claire Naval of the OECD Development Co-operation Directorate, Global Partnerships and Policies Division. The report was authored by the Global Initiative against Transnational Organized Crime (www.globalinitiative.net). The primary author, co-ordinator and editor is Tuesday Reitano, Deputy Director of the Global Initiative, with contributions from Karl Lallerstedt and Rob McCusker.*

Several authors prepared the case studies (to be published as separate working papers) and provided the background data for this report:

- Human smuggling from West Africa to Europe – Tuesday Reitano
- Illicit narcotics transiting West Africa – Mark Shaw
- Illicit trade in counterfeit and substandard goods in Ghana – Karl Lallerstedt
- The artisanal and small-scale gold-mining sector – Marcena Hunter
- Illicit financial flows and Al-Qaeda in the Islamic Maghreb – Theodore Kouts.

The team drew on the support of a team of Research Associates at the Global Initiative, including Iris Oustinoff, Adam Rodriques and Jessica Gerken. We also gratefully acknowledge the inputs of Lena Diesing (OECD Public Governance Directorate), Louis Marechal and Hannah Koep-Andrieu (OECD Directorate for Financial and Enterprise Affairs), and Jean-Christophe Dumont (OECD Directorate for Employment, Labour and Social Affairs).

We would like to thank the different peer reviewers who provided expertise at different stages of a rigorous peer-review process that allowed five forthcoming case studies and the full report to be reviewed separately:

Florence Dennis, Maimouna Diop Ly, Samuel Ijeh, Kevin Lumbila, Sanjeev Narrainen and Pietro Toigo (AfDB); Yves Bertran and Patrick Schein (Alliance for Responsible Mining); Eric Gutierrez (Christian Aid); Fabian Klemme, Florian Lewerenz, Mark Mattner and Manuel Papouschek (Deutsche Gesellschaft für Internationale Zusammenarbeit);

* The authors would like to dedicate this book to Professor Stephen Ellis (1953-2015), one of the foremost authorities on illicit economies in West Africa and an invaluable resource over the course of this study, both in person and through his vast collection of scholarly and policy works.

Anna Triandafyllidou (European University Institute); Shana Krishnan (Financial Action Task Force); Jeffrey Isima and Umar Muazu (GIABA); Louis Bonnier, Tracy Faustin and Suriya Prabha (International Chamber of Commerce Business Action to Stop Counterfeiting and Piracy; Claudia Natali and Vijaya Souri (International Organization for Migration); Florence Nazare and Bob Kalanzi (NEPAD Agency); Sara Batmanglich, Laure Brillaud, Dan Devlin, Jean-Christophe Dumont, Amy Hong, Louis Marechal, Kathryn Nwajiaku, Piotr Stryszowski and Bakary Traoré (OECD); Marie Tremolieres (Sahel and West Africa Club); Tom Keatinge (Royal United Services Institute); James Donovan (Swedish International Development Cooperation Agency); Phil Mason (United Kingdom Department for International Development); Adam Gardner and Joe Whittle (United Kingdom Home Office); Anga Timilsina (United Nations Development Programme); Roberto Sollazzo (United Nations Group of Experts on Côte d'Ivoire); Melissa Tullis (United Nations Organization on Drugs and Crime); Brooke Stearns Lawson (United States Agency for International Development); Anja P. Jakobi (Technische Universität Braunschweig); Mathieu Quet (Institut de Recherche pour le Développement); Thanos Maroukis (University of Bath); Attiya Waris (University of Nairobi); Olivier Walther (University of Southern Denmark); Joel A. Turkewitz and Andreas Seiter (World Bank); and Mariya Polner, Anca Elena Trefas and Sandra Wens (World Customs Organization).

Another group (referred to as a Reference Group) volunteered time and experience throughout 2015, providing access to key informants and guiding decisions related to the choice of case studies (to be published as Working Papers). The Reference Group included:

Wilfrid Abiola, Evelynne Change and Emanuele Santi (AfDB); Habiba Ben Barka (United Nations Economic Commission for Africa); Fabian Klemme (Deutsche Gesellschaft für Internationale Zusammenarbeit); Adeline Defer (Ministère des Affaires étrangères et du Développement international, France); Umar Muazu (GIABA); Stanley Ude (INTERPOL); Claire Delpeuch, Gregory de Paepe, Katie Johnston, Hannah Koep-Andrieu, Louis Marechal, Jack Radisch, Silvia Sorescu and Piotr Stryszowski (OECD); Marie Tremolieres (Sahel and West Africa Club); Phil Mason (United Kingdom Department for International Development); Anga Timilsina (United Nations Development Programme); Brooke Stearns Lawson (United States Agency for International Development); Larissa Alanna Gray and Emile van der Does de Willebois (Stolen Asset Recovery Initiative); and Melissa Tullis (United Nations Office on Drugs and Crime).

Cynthia Peck-Kubaczek, Philippa Garson, Mark Foss and Romy de Courtay provided editing and proofreading. Sharon Wilson created the graphics and artwork. A number of the infographic representations used icons provided by Freepik.com from Flaticon.com, licensed by Creative Commons BY 3.0.

About the authors

Tuesday Reitano Tuesday Reitano is the Deputy Director of the Global Initiative against Transnational Organized Crime (Global Initiative). She previously worked at the United Nations Office on Drugs and Crime, and the United Nations Development Programme, looking at the nexus of transnational threats, fragile states and development.

Karl Lallerstedt Karl Lallerstedt leads the Programme on Illicit Trade, Financial and Economic Crime at the Global Initiative. He is also the co-founder of the non-governmental organisation Black Market Watch (www.blackmarketwatch.org), which targets illicit trade. Karl was formerly the anti-illicit trade strategy director at a leading multinational corporation.

Rob McCusker Rob McCusker is the Transnational Crime Director at Gulf Vigilance, the former Director of the Centre for Fraud and Financial Crime at Teesside University, and the former transnational crime analyst for the Australian Institute of Criminology (a statutory agency within the portfolio of the Minister for Justice). Rob is a member of the Global Initiative Network of Experts.

Mark Shaw Mark Shaw is the Director of the Global Initiative against Transnational Organized Crime and a Visiting Senior Fellow at the London School of Economics, LSE IDEAS Drug Policy Programme. He recently served as the Chair of Criminology and Director of the Centre of Criminology at the Faculty of Law of the University of Cape Town (www.criminology.uct.ac.za), where he held the South African National Research Foundation Chair in Security and Justice.

Marcena Hunter Marcena Hunter is a Senior Research Analyst at the Global Initiative, with specialised expertise in understanding and responding to transnational organised crime and IFFs in the natural-resource sector. She has a background in transnational justice and rule of law, international human-rights standards and norms, and sustainable development, among other issues.

Theodore Kouts Theodore Kouts is a consultant at the World Bank in Finance and Markets, specialising in and authoring research on terrorist financing issues. He received a Master of Letters degree in Terrorism Studies from the University of St. Andrews, a Master of Science degree in Crime Scene Investigation from George Washington University, and a Bachelor of Arts degree in Criminology and Criminal Justice with a minor in Terrorism Studies from the University of Maryland.

Table of contents

Tables

Figures

Abbreviations and acronyms

AfDB	African Development Bank
AML	Anti-money laundering
2030 Agenda	2030 Agenda for Sustainable Development
AQIM	Al-Qaeda in the Islamic Maghreb
ASGM	Artisanal and small-scale gold mining
CFA	West African CFA franc (currency)
CFT	Countering the financing of terrorism
DCD	OECD Development Co-operation Directorate
ECA	Economic Commission for Africa
ECOWAS	Economic Community of West African States
EEZ	Exclusive economic zone
EU	European Union
FATF	Financial Action Task Force
FIU	Financial Intelligence Unit
GDP	Gross domestic product
GIABA	Inter-Governmental Action Group against Money Laundering in West Africa
HDI	Human Development Index
HLP	High Level Panel on Illicit Financial Flows from Africa
IC3	US Internet Complaint Center
IFFs	Illicit financial flows
IIAG	Ibrahim Index of African Governance
ILO	International Labour Organization
IOM	International Organization for Migration
IUU	Illegal, unreported and unregulated
KFR	Kidnap for ransom
MTO	Money transfer operator
NGO	Non-governmental organisation

NEPAD	New Partnership for Africa's Development
ODA	Official development assistance
OECD	Organisation for Economic Co-operation and Development
PEPs	Politically exposed persons
t/d	Metric tonnes per day
UEMOA	Union Économique et Monétaire Ouest Africaine
UN	United Nations
UNHCR	United Nations High Commissioner for Refugees
UNODC	United Nations Office on Drugs and Crime
UNSC	United Nations Security Council
UNTOC	United Nations Convention against Transnational Organized Crime
USD	US dollar
WACD	West Africa Commission on Drugs
WHO	World Health Organization
WHO IMPACT	World Health Organization's International Medical Products Anti-Counterfeiting Taskforce

Executive summary

Africa is the world's second fastest-growing economy after East Asia, and yet the continent is also home to the largest share of people living in extreme poverty, in countries with poor foundations for human development. Income inequality is rising, while underemployment and the lack of economic opportunities push some individuals to join criminal groups, gangs or rebel movements, reinforcing the links between inequality, criminal activity and violence.

The United Nations Economic Commission for Africa's High Level Panel on Illicit Financial Flows has estimated that illicit financial flows (IFFs) from Africa could amount to as much as USD 50 billion (US dollars) per year. Although the figures on IFFs are heavily disputed, current analyses agree that IFFs exceed the amount of ODA provided to Africa.

Previous research has largely focused on capturing the volumes and sources of IFFs, and on identifying the commercial practices that contribute to them such as trade misinvoicing, tax evasion and avoidance, and transfer pricing.

This publication takes a different approach by seeking to build the evidence basis on criminal and illicit economies, the IFFs these economies generate, and their impact on development. The report reviews diverse forms of economies prevalent in West Africa that are usually seen as criminal or illicit, organising them through a typology according to a range of illegal activities, from natural resource crimes to illicit trade in normally legal goods.

This analysis leads to the following conclusions: criminal and illicit economies produce IFFs that undermine country capacities to finance their development; and criminal economies and IFFs are a potent negative force that contribute to the degradation of livelihoods and ecosystems, undermine institutions, reinforce clientelist politics and enable impunity, in different ways across the region's countries.

Key findings

Criminal acts are enabled by a diverse set of actors, including criminal networks, the private sector (both domestic and international), and state officials. Criminal methods are dynamic processes, changing in response to opportunities, and to global and local market forces.

IFFs and criminality erode the fabric of the state across the region, and often cause politics, business and crime to converge, creating ambiguity around governance and rule of law. Certain criminal and illicit economies in the region carry low levels of stigma within communities, as they are an important source of livelihood, building legitimacy that enables alternative governance providers to compete with the state and create alternate sources of authority.

The licit and illicit are increasingly interwoven in West Africa. This is partly due to the size of the informal economy, which is estimated to constitute as much as 60-70% of total economic activity in the region. It is also a product of the elite protection networks connected to licit and illicit flows. Money flows to local powerbrokers, as well as armed, criminal and terrorist groups, as it would (should) flow to the state.

Low levels of financial inclusion further facilitate the environment for criminal economies and IFFs in the region. Access to the formal banking system is out of reach for many. Money transfer operators, the principal means of remittance exchange and international financial transactions in the West Africa, are prohibitively expensive. Consequently, transactions are often conducted in cash, or through informal systems of money transfer, placing significant volumes of transactions outside the reach of government, regulators and international trade measurement.

Given the scope of criminal economies in the region, and the relatively low level of capacity and resources available to address them, understanding their local livelihood contributions and setting priorities to address them is key to successfully combatting them.

Conclusions and recommendations

Criminal economies interact depending on three factors: whether the good is sourced locally or externally; who are the actors and networks involved; and how IFFs are earned and where they are invested. The analysis leads to the following broad findings:

- Informal activities generating IFFs that remain in the region cannot always be stigmatised as criminal.
- Criminal industries driven by natural resources whose IFFs are invested outside of the region present the most significant net losses.
- Transit-trade goods with a limited local market are most likely to induce high-level corruption and protection network, commensurate with their value.
- Criminal economies with a significant local market are most likely to play into local power hierarchies, potentially leading to insecurity, violence and conflict.

In this study, both regional and international law-enforcement officials highlighted that development and governance concerns seriously constrain their ability to address criminal enterprises effectively. These concerns include instability; limited state authority or presence; communities and cities with a strong dependence on smuggling as a livelihood strategy; long and porous borders that make credible border enforcement impossible; and weak institutions with limited capacity, resources or political support for sustained investigations.

According to the 2030 Agenda, addressing organised crime and IFFs is the responsibility of development actors. The responsibility is twofold: addressing criminal economies, and the socio-economic and governance conditions that produce or increase them; and mitigating the impacts of criminal economies on a country's trajectory of development.

The close linkages between people, economies and territories in West Africa ensure that unilateral action can only have limited impact, displacing rather than reducing criminal economies and IFFs. At the same time, not all activities are strictly illegal, and not all illicit activities are stigmatised as criminal by the individuals affected. Measured and targeted responses are needed according to the level of harm that may result from the activity in question.

The struggle to combat IFFs is also a struggle that crosses boundaries. Although focusing its analysis on West African countries, this report recognises the joint responsibility of countries of origin, transit and destination. Accordingly, it calls on OECD and African countries to take coherent and coordinated policy action to ensure that each country entwined in the IFF economy plays its part to reduce the opportunity for criminal activity and IFFs, and protect vulnerable populations from their damaging impacts.

Chapter 1.

Overview

The negative impact of illicit financial flows (IFFs) on development goals increasingly features on international political agendas. This publication seeks to build evidence on IFFs and their impact, by looking at the relationship between criminal and illicit economies, and their generated revenue in West Africa. The report moves beyond traditional efforts to measure IFFs towards developing a qualitative understanding of how these activities affect the economy, governance, development and human security. It proposes a framework for analysing the diverse ways in which these economies and IFFs threaten development and human security for West African citizens and states. It concludes with recommendations to develop an integrated response to these activities and the networks that perpetuate them, which addresses the enabling environment and seeks to mitigate their impacts on the most vulnerable populations.

Why look at criminal economies and illicit financial flows in West Africa?

Illicit financial flows (IFFs), defined as "money illegally earned, transferred or used" (United Nations Economic Commission for Africa [ECA], 2013), are increasingly understood as a threat to sustainable development and one of the greatest contemporary challenges to global development. They undercut economic growth and legitimate trade, depriving governments of the financial resources they might otherwise invest in public goods, such as health, education and infrastructure. IFFs carry a high price, as they are often concomitant with the illicit-arms trade, drug trafficking and the commodities resourcing conflict. IFFs are particularly prevalent and damaging in the context of developing, institutionally weak and fragile states, where they tend to exploit and exacerbate weaknesses in public institutions, undermine governance and empower those who operate outside of the law.

Because they present a significant threat to security, stability and development, IFFs have increasingly featured on the agenda of leading political initiatives, such as the Group of Eight and the Group of Twenty. For its part, the OECD Strategy on Development (2012) identified IFFs as one of its three priorities, central to its mandate "to promote policies that will improve the economic and social well-being of people around the world" (OECD, 2012).

The OECD has published research on IFFs, with the understanding that combatting the phenomenon would increase the resources available for development. The report on *Illicit Financial Flows from Developing Countries: Measuring OECD Responses* (OECD, 2014a), for example, compares the performance of OECD member countries on a range of relevant international standards. The present study offers policy makers an analysis of another set of activities generating IFFs: criminal economies. It situates this theme within a development context to synthesise and deepen the existing analysis. In so doing, it helps policy makers understand the scale and impact of such activities, and the resulting IFFs in West Africa.

The African continent remains the second fastest-growing economy in the world: several African countries (Côte d'Ivoire, Djibouti, Ethiopia, Rwanda and United Republic of Tanzania) post growth rates between 6% and 10% (African Development Bank [AfDB]/OECD/United Nations Development Programme [UNDP], 2016). Historically, it receives the highest proportion of official development assistance (ODA) globally (Figure 1.1). Yet while the poverty rate has declined, the number of people in living in extreme poverty has increased substantially since the 1990s, due to population growth (World Bank, 2016): three out of four Africans still live in a country with poor foundations for human development, compared to one in five globally (AfDB/OECD/UNDP, 2016).[1] Income inequality is also rising, affecting the social consensus required to adjust to major shocks and increasing the volatility of economic growth (Ostry, Berg, and Tsangarides, 2014). Countries with higher income inequality tend to experience more homicides; underemployment and lack of opportunity are among the primary reasons young people join gangs, criminal groups or rebel movements, reinforcing the links between inequality and violence. Repeated cycles of violence – whether from conflict or crime – have been estimated to reduce development performance by 20% (World Bank, 2011).

Within the continent, West Africa[2] arguably experiences the negative impacts of illicit flows most acutely. Lower development indicators, weak state institutions and limited regulatory capacity allow resources to be diverted and illegal acts to thrive, undermining the integrity of institutions through corruption. In some countries, corruption has impaired the rule of law, and the relationship between citizens and the state.

Figure 1.1.**Bilateral ODA by region**

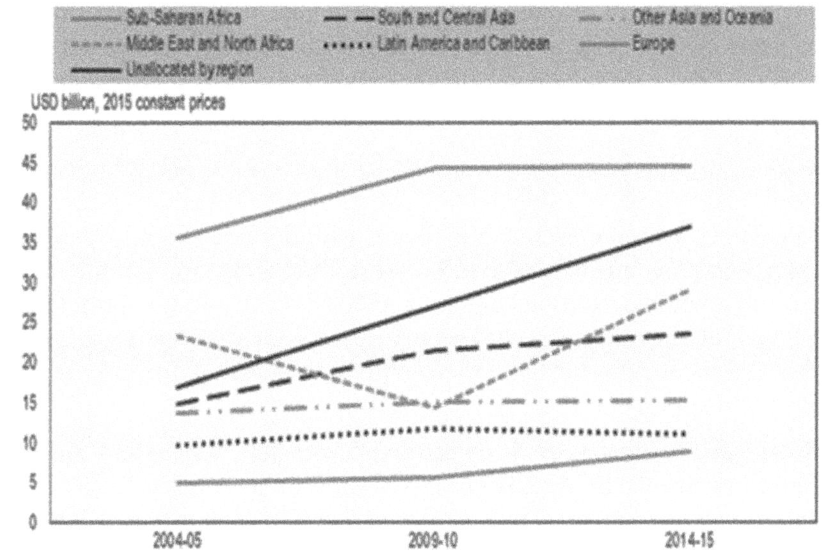

Source: OECD statistics.

Across the continent, IFFs have been proven to resource conflicts and groups with terrorist agendas. A criminal economy in its own right, the illegal arms trade has also chronically exacerbated human insecurity and increased violence levels within communities. According to the United Nations, the continent posts some of the highest levels of homicide in the world (United Nations Office on Drugs and Crime [UNODC], 2014). Firms in sub-Saharan Africa lose a higher percentage of sales to illicit trade and crime, and spend a higher percentage of sales on security, than any other region (World Bank, 2011).

Renewed attention to IFFs has generated a positive momentum to curb illicit flows in Africa, as evidenced by the African Union's commitment to halve IFFs by 2023 (New Partnership for Africa's Development [NEPAD Agency], 2014). At the same time, the OECD Development Assistance Committee's work on IFFs in Africa, and West Africa in particular, recognises the shared responsibility of OECD member countries, as transit or recipient countries, to help partner countries address criminal economies, as well as reduce IFFs and protect the vulnerable from their damaging impacts.

Structure of the report

Based on a literature and data review, the first three chapters provide insights into foundational issues. Chapter 1 presents the overall report and the situation in West Africa. Chapter 2 provides an overview of the region's key characteristics, and describes how vulnerabilities facilitate criminal economies and illicit trade. Chapter 3 provides an analytical framework for understanding the different forms of harm arising from criminal and illicit economies. It also examines 13 different forms of criminal economies according to a three-part typology: illegal activities, illicit trade in legal goods and illicit resource extraction. Each case provides an overview of the scale of the flow and geographic area of vulnerability, the key actors involved, and the implications and development impacts of the IFFs they generate. Chapter 4 draws the major conclusions. It provides sectoral recommendations to international, regional and national actors to assist to create an environment – in the region and elsewhere – that is less conducive to criminal economies, and proposes measures to reduce these activities and their impact. In so doing, the report develops a framework for the holistic assessment of the harm resulting from criminal economies and related IFFs to West Africa's development. This framework can guide international actors and national governments in understanding and responding to these processes.

Scope and definitions

The lexicon around criminal economies and IFFs is not well defined. Terms are often used interchangeably, obscuring the nuances relevant to designing appropriate policy and development assistance. Even when definitions can be agreed, the capacity to apply them consistently may still prove challenging. As this report applies these terms to a broad scope of activities across a large geographic area, there will understandably be grey areas. The following definitions will apply:

Illicit financial flows (IFFs): this term is used in its broadest sense, as "money illegally earned, transferred or used" (ECA, 2013).[3] Discussion of IFFs often focuses on their measurement in relation to commercial tax-payment issues. In this report, IFFs are understood as the revenue and proceeds generated by the following activities:

- corruption: the proceeds of theft, bribery, graft and embezzlement of national wealth by government officials
- commerce: the proceeds of tax evasion, misrepresentation, misreporting and misinvoicing related to trade activities, and money laundering through commercial transactions
- crime: the proceeds of criminal activities, including drug trafficking, smuggling, counterfeiting, racketeering (also known as criminal protection or extortion) and terrorist financing (ECA, 2013).

Of course, the balance between these three forms of IFFs differs substantially from country to country. West Africa is deeply affected by corruption and clientelism. However, these issues manifest differently, depending on the extent of the natural resource or export sector (Benassi et al., 2015) and the nature of the illicit flows transiting the country. Typically, higher value illicit flows, such as the trade of narcotics, tend to correlate with higher levels of corruption.

Traditional analyses of IFFs generally focus on discussing their volume, and do not address the extensive, multidimensional nature of the harm caused by criminal economies. IFF analyses also tend to capture their value and impact solely in monetary terms granting more importance to the highest-value outflows. Often, they do not examine other types of illicit activities that may have a greater and more damaging development impacts. For example, cocaine trafficking throughout the region may represent a criminal flow worth over USD 3 billion annually. Its impact, however, arguably pales in comparison to the extensive damage to ecosystems and livelihoods wreaked by illegal fishing in the Gulf of Guinea, a criminal flow worth USD 1.2 billion. Others may observe that although the trade in kidnapping for ransom has generated only around USD 100 million in the last decade, its impact is manifold, as it has directly resourced terrorist groups. Thus, although understanding harm may always be subjective, it is an important analytical exercise that affects the setting of response priorities.

A second challenge deriving from the way IFFs are understood is that the term itself can predefine a set of responses focused on controlling monetary flows, limiting the potential for alternate programmatic or policy responses. For example, policy makers could become intent on strengthening law enforcement or border control and increasing regulation over the financial sector; however, as security and law enforcement officials themselves have noted – and as this study concludes – these interventions can only prove minimally effective within West Africa's socio-economic and political framework. In a region where the informal sector dominates the economy, where mobility between states is both a citizenship right and a resilience strategy, and where capacity for regulation over borders and transactions is weak, and corruption and impunity are widespread, such interventions are hamstrung. Instead, holistic strategies are required to target those who control criminal enterprises, by studying and breaking down the networks and vested interests that perpetuate these criminal and illicit activities. This will involve analysing the actors and interests – from the level of the community, to the nation state, the region and internationally – associated with global transnational flows, and then co-ordinating and harmonising responses.

Another key finding of this report is that weak policy coherence across the region fuels criminal economies and those who control them. Relevant policy areas include trade and subsidy regimes, as well as criminal justice systems and penalties. As is the case in the rest of the world, criminal networks in Africa can move flexibly among countries, markets and commodities; they search for an environment where they can operate more easily thanks to weaker state institutions, and can acquire legitimacy and support from local communities.

Criminal economy: this report uses the term "criminal economies" broadly, referring not only to activities that are clearly illegal, but also to others that are illicit but include some subsistence component (as discussed in the case study on artisanal and small-scale gold mining [ASGM]). With respect to "trade transactions", the report refers both to illegal goods (such as narcotic drugs) and legal goods that break regulations during circulation. As used in this report, the term entails a component of illegality at some stage in the process – perhaps in the way the goods were sourced or produced, or the manner in which they became illegal in the commercial supply chain (e.g. through theft, diversion or misrepresentation). The report refers to the revenues generated by these economies as IFFs.

The report is structured around a typology of three forms of criminal economies: illegal activities, illicit trade in normally legal goods and illicit resource extraction (Table 1.1). This typology is more fully explained, and applied to a range of criminal economies, in Chapter 3.

The definition of a "criminal economy" includes a number of criminal practices and commodities, such as the trade in stolen oil and cocaine. Although oil is a legal good, trading in stolen oil is an illegal activity that generates IFFs; it reduces government revenue, binds labour in illegal activities and ignores regulations supposed to protect citizens. Cocaine, on the other hand, is clearly illegal, as is the trade in the drug. Not only can the state not legitimately claim taxes over it, it also exacts an additional economic cost because the state deploys resources to respond to the trade that could have been used for other purposes. Services and certain intangible practices can also generate criminal economies and IFFs. For example, Internet-enabled crimes and identity theft are criminal practices that have economic consequences; they are also included within the definition of IFFs.

Table 1.1. **Typology of criminal economies**

	Illegal activities	Illicit trade in legal goods	Illicit resource extraction
Definition	Activities or commodities that are illegal in all contexts (or, in the case of drug trafficking, are illegal except when used for specific purposes, i.e. medical or scientific purposes); thus, any association with their trade is illegal by default.	Activities that relate to resources predominantly sourced outside of the region, and for which West African countries are a destination or major transit zone.	Activities that relate to resources sourced in the region that are inherently legal, and for which government control and taxation would be expected in normal circumstances, but which have never entered the formal economy, or have moved into the illicit economy at some point between source and market.
Examples	Drug trafficking Kidnapping for ransom Human trafficking Smuggling of migrants Counterfeiting Cybercrime/fraud Maritime piracy	Illicit tobacco Arms smuggling Commodity smuggling	Illicit mining Oil bunkering Environmental crimes (including illegal, unreported and unregulated fishing)

Organised crime: although little consensus exists on the application of the term "organised crime", it is widely used. Money laundering – i.e. the means through which profits from illicit activity enter the formal or legitimate economy – is typically included within the definition of organised crime. This report, however, focuses on IFFs; hence, money laundering is more relevant as a means to an end, rather than as an end in itself. The issue sits at the nexus between criminal economies and IFFs, and thus will be considered within the context of the proceeds of illicit trade.

A distinction also needs to be drawn between what constitutes an organised criminal act, practice or flow and an organised-crime group. Article 2(a) of the United Nations Convention against Transnational Organized Crime (UNTOC) defines an organised-crime group as "a group of three or more persons that was not randomly formed; existing for a period of time; acting in concert with the aim of at least one crime punishable by at least four years' incarceration; in order to obtain, directly or indirectly, a financial or other material benefit" (UNTOC, 2004).

This definition has limitations, particularly in the context of Africa, where insurgent or militia groups using illicit resources for political motivations overlap, and where the existing national laws may not criminalise certain acts. It may be the case that activities – typically within the informal economy – that are perceived as criminal at the international level do not carry the same stigma with communities, as they represent an important source of livelihoods and are considered a form of entrepreneurship (Ellis and Shaw, 2015). This local support base may enable alternative governance providers to compete with the state and create alternative sources of authority, particularly among groups – such as minority ethnic groups, immigrants in urban hubs and remote communities – lacking access to public services and protection (Felbab-Brown, 2013; Reitano and Hunter, 2016).

Analysis on the issue of organised crime has splintered into two primary frameworks: the study of the commodity flows and the study of the groups controlling these flows. Arguably, those seeking to prevent certain commodities from entering a market will find it more effective to analyse the flows of illicit commodities and trade as a whole, rather than the individual groups along the value chain, from production and transit to destination. However, understanding the impact of illicit trade in specific areas – e.g. governance or insecurity – requires analysing the interaction of individuals and groups with those criminal activities in a localised context. To be relevant for local policy making and implementation, the understanding needs to be quite specific and granular, and considered in a given country context. This report aims to draw higher level conclusions and is not intended to achieve that level of country-specific detail.

Distinguishing between organised crime and other criminal behaviour can be useful, and the issue of scale is important. This report is more concerned with organised crime and criminal economies that meet the UNTOC definition (provided above). As such, it discusses subsistence-level criminal activity (e.g. poaching for individual use or *ad hoc* facilitation of illicit migration) from the perspective of the impact of that subsistence activity on the nation's economy or socio-political fabric.

Informal economy: under the OECD definition, the informal economy includes all economic actors whose activities primarily focus on generating employment or income for themselves alone (OECD, n.d.; International Labour Organization, 1993). This includes activities at a subsistence level or for personal use, such as cash paid for domestic services. The emphasis in using this term, however, is generally not on intentionally illegal activities. Rather, it typically encompasses those activities the local community may not perceive as criminal, such as cross-border smuggling of basic foodstuffs, which predominantly contribute to subsistence livelihoods. In 2010, the Inter-Governmental Action Group against Money Laundering in West Africa (GIABA) estimated that the informal economy accounted for an average of 60-70% of total economic activity across the region (Financial Action Task Force [FATF] & GIABA, 2013).

The criminal economies of West Africa

This report focuses on several criminal economies in West Africa, ranging from ASGM or trading in counterfeit goods, which are so widespread they are better considered informal industries rather than criminal practices, to drug trafficking, which are always deemed a serious and organised crime at an international scale. Some West African actors are lead agents in industries such as cybercrime and advance-fee fraud. In other industries, such as trafficking in methamphetamines or enabling illicit extraction of the region's plentiful natural resources, they are capturing an increasingly important share of the global supply chain.

Numerous systemic factors, related to the region's geography, demography and socio-economic conditions, enable criminal economies. They are further exacerbated by weak states and governance, including through clientelism, elite resource capture, corruption and impunity. Not only have cycles of conflict and fragility in specific subregions created displacement, fragility and insecurity, they have also opened up space for insurgencies and ethnic conflict to develop into violent extremism. Citizens' disenfranchisement from the state, as well as states' inability to provide dividends on citizenship, have given legitimacy to local powerbrokers, armed groups and fundamentalist ideologies. In turn, the paucity of legitimate livelihoods has enhanced the role of criminal economies (some of them informal livelihoods) and the groups enabling them.

Despite the diversity of the activities considered in this report, a number of common conclusions can be drawn, particularly about how West Africa has become more vulnerable to illicit activity, without significant capacity to address them. First, the distinction between "licit" and "illicit" is often blurred, partly owing to the expansive nature of the informal economy generating livelihoods for most of the region's citizens. Whole communities may depend on specific forms of illicit trade. On the Sahel borders, this might be commodity and fuel smuggling; in agricultural zones, it might be illicit logging or forced labour sponsoring specific industries, such as cocoa production. With few viable legitimate livelihood opportunities within the formal economy, these other forms of trade and industry – albeit illicit – are subsistence-level activities; they are not criminalised, but rather considered as informal economic enterprises. The profits are generated and invested in basic services and operations within the local community, generating a series of collateral services – including accommodation, food provision and armed security for hire – supporting the industry. This amplifies the benefits of illicit trade and fosters economic dependency on the part of the community. However, subsistence-level activities are more susceptible to predatory behaviour from criminal groups seeking to capture rents and profits, and to extort those working in the informal economy.

Second, individuals engaged in criminal economies and encouraged by the lack of stigma associated with illegal acts are free to parlay their IFFs into political power. Due to the clientelist nature of local and central governments across West Africa, the ability to secure rents and provide livelihoods – whether licit or illicit – can translate into local authority and legitimacy, further blurring the lines (Alemika, 2013). Clientelism, combined with the lack of stigma, transparency and oversight, has translated into a culture of impunity for criminal associations: key figures in business and government can operate within the legitimate and illegitimate economy without censure. They serve as a fulcrum, enabling criminal economies, shifting funds between the licit and illicit economy, and making connections to influential figures. In this way, illicit enterprises hijack the physical and financial infrastructure of legitimate trade in West Africa, and both governance and electoral politics become invested in protecting the interests of criminals rather than citizens.

At one end of the spectrum is elite capture of criminal rents. At the other end, the ability to levy taxes on both licit and illicit trade is increasingly falling outside of the purview of West African central states. Charging for protection – in other words, extortion – is one strategy of criminal groups involved in drug trafficking and other forms of illegal behaviour, and can enrich armed militias involved in the region's conflict systems, as well as terrorist groups. Across the region, the profits of trade flow to local powerbrokers, instead of to the central state. Protection becomes a commodity in itself, and the use of violence plays a pivotal role in the fight for control.

Finally, low levels of financial inclusion are a major contributor to the enabling environment for criminal economies and IFFs in West Africa. Access to the formal banking system is out of reach for the majority of ordinary people. Money transfer operators (MTOs), the principal means for international remittance exchange and transacting, are prohibitively expensive. This has created a demand for alternative systems operating outside of government regulation, reducing the efficacy of Financial Intelligence Units, and increasing the risks of money laundering and terrorist financing.

Towards a framework for understanding criminal economies and IFFs

This report highlights that existing approaches do not capture the relations between IFFs and criminal economies. In particular, it notes that Goal 16.4 of the 2030 Agenda for Sustainable Development (ASD 2030)[4] requires development actors to respond to the challenges of organised crime and IFFs. With this in mind, it proposes a framework for analysing and prioritising responses, based upon a wider analysis of harm revolving around five areas crucial to development:

- **Physical harm** is harm to persons (homicides, violent crime) or physical infrastructure (damage to property).
- **Societal harm** creates or exacerbates societal tensions (including inciting violent conflict, and ethnic, gender-based or inter-generational conflict or violence), as well as economic or social marginalisation.
- **Economic harm** in the form of direct and indirect harm to the economy. Directly, IFFs withdraw funds from the legitimate economy; they may incite the state to divert resources in order to prevent and respond to criminally motivated harms, or treat or compensate its victims. Indirectly, IFFs damage the economic climate, competitiveness, and investment and entrepreneurship cultures.
- **Environmental harm** is caused by unsustainable use of environmental resources and the by-products of criminal activity.
- **Structural/governance harm** is damage done to the quality of the governance or rule-of-law system as a result of corruption, and through the erosion of the state's reputation, legitimacy and authority.

These harms can be analysed and felt at the individual, community, national and international levels, with differences based on demographics, gender and specific vulnerable groups.

The proposed framework suggests using these areas of harm as a filter through which to gauge the impact of specific criminal economies. Three sets of questions, derived from the analysis in this report, can guide this assessment of impacts:

1. Where is the good sourced, and is there a local market?
2. Who are the actors and networks involved?
3. Where are the IFFs earned and invested?

These questions add value because, when analysed congruently, they allow stakeholders to better understand the extent and nature of the harm stemming from illicit and criminal activities. This report analysed criminal economies through a typology that isolated illicit financial flows and activities derived from commodities indigenous to the region from those sourced elsewhere.

The first question is relevant both for goods sourced in the region and goods sourced externally. It helps understand the extent of local communities' vested interest in perpetuating the commodity flow, and encourages reflection on whether the groups trafficking these goods have gained legitimacy. When applied to externally sourced goods, this question also helps determine how this illicit commodity flow might affect the legitimate economy. Answering the first question, the analysis showed that many criminal economies in West Africa (illicit fishing, illicit logging, wildlife trafficking and resource diversion in the extractive industries, including oil theft) centre on indigenous natural resources, including flora and fauna. Their diversion represents a loss of potential benefit to the region's citizens, and often correlates with practices that are damaging to the environment or unsafe for those engaged in them.

The second question is an important political-economy consideration that examines the underlying agency and incentives associated with the given activity: who is involved (e.g. public, private, entrepreneurial or criminal interests; regional, communal, or even faith-based actors), how heavily invested they may be in the activity, and the extent of their control and influence.

The final question highlights a key finding of this report: the impact of criminal economies – and thus the responses required – differ considerably, depending on where the IFF generated by the criminal economy is earned and invested. This examination of the different forms of criminal economies found that IFFs that remain in the community, country or region contribute to informal economic activity, regardless of how they are earned and even if they are outright illegal (e.g. cybercrime). Understood in this way, they should be seen as a distorting market force impacting on legitimate industries and the formal sector. At the same time, they generate income locally, which will grow the economy as a whole and create livelihood opportunities.

Based on the analysis above, those IFFs that generate local income demand protection – possibly through violence or civil protest – from the individuals or entities to whom the income accrues. Moreover, criminal economies with local markets and locally invested IFFs play into local power hierarchies, resourcing and strengthening those controlling the flow, whether a terrorist group or a local politician. By contrast, those industries – such as natural-resource extraction – where the IFFs are mostly accrued or invested abroad have an entirely different dynamic. The extraction of goods indigenous to the region is a net loss to the state and its citizens. This is particularly true where the goods are a finite resource, and the impact on the environment or sustainability of a species could be irreversible. Goods that pass through countries without a local market and the limited IFFs generated and invested in the region tend to contribute to elite corruption at a scale commensurate with the value of the flow.

Recommendations

The analysis of this report on the region's susceptibility to criminal economies makes it clear that IFFs are a development problem. The international community has tended to rely too heavily on law enforcement, border control and judicial strategies as the primary response to cross-border threats and criminal economies. However, both regional and international law-enforcement officials interviewed for this report clearly stated that development concerns seriously constrain their ability to address criminal enterprises effectively. These issues include instability; limited state authority or presence; communities and cities for which smuggling is a livelihood strategy, and which present strong economic dependence on those industries; long and porous borders that make credible border enforcement impossible; and limited capacity, resources or political support for sustained investigations.

Several conditions are also needed to ensure effective security responses by law enforcement: developing sustainable livelihoods; promoting the rule of law; enhancing financial inclusion; reducing corruption; and strengthening the capacity and development orientation of the state and state institutions. Leadership by national governments needs to be the primary driver of any kind of response, as reducing or returning IFFs will fail to translate into development benefits for ordinary people if elite corruption persists.

At the same time, given regional interdependencies and the transnational nature of the flow, ECOWAS countries need to work together on common strategies, policies, legislation, taxation and subsidy regimes. Regional approaches are essential, as differences between states create opportunities for criminal economies to develop and move to new countries or subregions, and those strategies need to be followed up with concrete implementation, underpinned by sufficient resources and political will. Strategies and legislation in the West African region are often adequate for responding to criminal practices, but their implementation falls short. Understandably, given the number of criminal economies, and the relatively low level of capacity and resources available to address them, setting priorities will be key to achieving results. The framework outlined in this report is one tool to help prioritise responses, based on the harm and negative impact on the region.

Achieving results in combatting criminal economies also requires support and action in transit and destination countries, including OECD member countries. West Africa is only one part of a global supply chain of illicit goods and services. Many activities centre on commodities produced elsewhere. It is not credible to expect West African states to address these economies in isolation; the responsibility is shared among source, transit and destination countries. Often, markets in OECD member countries drive demand.

Commonly accepted behavioural norms can be changed. This can occur through both legal and judicial means, as well as through market incentives and disincentives (which can be further reinforced by social pressure). By leveraging both state and non-state actors, and working at international and local levels, exposure, awareness raising and activism can promote or discourage behaviour, and signal that "business as usual" cannot continue. This report's findings highlight the need to bring a full set of instruments to the table, including not only legislative and criminal-justice instruments, but also economic and trade policy, as well as classic development interventions that reinforce stability, foster socio-economic growth, and promote governance and the rule of law.

Notes

1. Per the UNDP (2016), the Human Development Index (HDI) is a summary measure of average achievement in key dimensions of human development: a long and healthy life, being knowledgeable and have a decent standard of living. The HDI is the geometric mean of normalised indices for each of the three dimensions. The health dimension is assessed by life expectancy at birth, the education dimension is measured by the mean of years of schooling for adults aged 25 years and more and the expected years of schooling is measured for children of school-entering age. The standard-of-living dimension is measured by gross national income per capita. The scores for the three HDI dimension indices are then aggregated into a composite index, using the geometric mean.
2. Specifically, the report addresses the 15 countries covered by the Economic Community of West African States (ECOWAS): Benin, Burkina Faso, Cabo Verde, Côte d'Ivoire, Gambia, Ghana, Guinea, Guinea-Bissau, Liberia, Mali, Niger, Nigeria, Senegal, Sierra Leone and Togo.
3. The term "capital flight" is often used synonymously with IFFs, but this is misleading. Capital flight is commonly understood as the moment capital or resources leave the domestic economy/jurisdiction to secure more favourable returns, which are then not reinvested or returned. This process can be legal or illegal, but will broadly be detrimental to the domestic economy (ECA, 2013).
4. The 2030 Agenda for Sustainable Development, the successor development framework to the Millennium Development Goals promulgated by the 193 Member

States of the United Nations in September 2015 (A/Res/70/1), lays out a series of transformative goals and targets that are perceived as central to achieving the United Nation's core goals of achieving peace, eradicating poverty and ensuring sustainable development for all peoples (www.un.org/ga/search/view_doc.asp?symbol=A/RES/70/1&Lang=E).

References

AfDB/OECD/UNDP (2016), *African Economic Outlook 2016: Sustainable Cities and Structural Transformation*, OECD Publishing, Paris, http://dx.doi.org/10.1787/aeo-2016-en.

Alemika, E. (2013), *The Impact of Organised Crime on Governance in West Africa,* Friedrich Ebert Stiftung, Abuja, http://library.fes.de/pdf-files/bueros/nigeria/10199.pdf.

Benassi, S. et al. (2015), *Algeria-Mali Trade: The Normality of Informality*, World Bank, Washington, DC, http://documents.worldbank.org/curated/en/839641468186541299/Algeria-Mali-trade-the-normality-of-informality.

ECA (2013), *The State of Governance in Africa: The Dimension of Illicit Financial Flows as a Development Challenge*, United Nations Economic Commission for Africa, Addis Ababa, www1.uneca.org/Portals/cgpp/2013/CGPP-3_Illicit-Financial-Flow-English_Final.pdf.

Ellis, S. and M. Shaw (2015), "Does organised crime exist in Africa?", *African Affairs*, Vol. 114/457, Oxford Journals, Oxford, http://dx.doi.org/10.1093/afraf/adv035.

FATF and GIABA (2013), *Report on Terrorist Financing in West Africa*, Financial Action Task Force/Inter-Governmental Action Group against Money Laundering in West Africa, Dakar.

Felbab-Brown, V. (2010), "The West African drug trade in context of the region's illicit economies and poor governance", paper presented to the Conference on Drug Trafficking in West Africa, Arlington, 4 October 2010, www.brookings.edu/research/speeches/2010/10/14-africa-drug-trade-felbabbrown.

ILO (1993), *Resolutions Concerning Statistics of Employment in the Informal Sector adopted by the 15th International Conference of Labour Statisticians*, January 1993, para. 5, International Labour Organization, Geneva.

NEPAD Agency (2014), *Africa Action Plan on Development Effectiveness*, NEPAD Agency, Addis Ababa, Ethiopia, www.nepad.org/resource/africa-action-plan-development-effectiveness.

OECD (2014a), *Illicit Financial Flows from Developing Countries: Measuring OECD Responses*, OECD Publishing, Paris. http://dx.doi.org/10.1787/9789264203501-en.

OECD (2014b), *Development Aid at a Glance: 2014*, OECD Publishing, Paris, www.oecd.org/dac/financing-sustainable-development/development-finance-data/aid-at-a-glance.htm.

OECD (2012), *OECD Strategy on Development*, OECD, Paris, www.oecd.org/pcd/OECD%20Development%20Strategy.pdf.

OECD (n.d), "Glossary of Statistical Terms", webpage, https://stats.oecd.org/glossary/detail.asp?ID=1350 (accessed 14 February 2016).

Ostry, J., A. Berg and C. Tsangarides (2014), *Redistribution, inequality, and Growth*, IMF Staff Discussion Note, International Monetary Fund, Washington, DC.

Reitano, T. and M. Hunter (2016), *Contests and Compacts: Organised Crime and Service Delivery*, International IDEA, Stockholm.

UNDP (2016), *Human Development Report 2016: Human Development for Everyone*, United Nations Development Programme, New York, http://hdr.undp.org/sites/default/files/2016_human_development_report.pdf.

UNODC (2014), *Global Study on Homicide 2013*, United Nations Office on Drugs and Crime, Vienna.

UNTOC (2004), *United Nations Convention against Transnational Organized Crime*, United Nations, New York.

World Bank (2016), *Poverty and Shared Prosperity 2016: Taking on Inequality*, World Bank, Washington, DC, https://doi.org/10.1596/978-1-4648-0958-3.

World Bank (2011), *World Development Report 2011*, World Bank, Washington, DC.

Further reading

Cockayne (2011), *State Fragility, Organised Crime and Peacebuilding: Towards a More Strategic Approach*, NOREF Report, Oslo.

Ellis, S. (2009), "West Africa's international drug trade", *African Affairs*, Vol. 108/431, Oxford Journals, Oxford, pp. 171-196, https://doi.org/10.1093/afraf/adp017.

OECD/World Bank (2014), *Few and Far: The Hard Facts on Stolen Asset Recovery*, World Bank, Washington, DC, http://dx.doi.org/10.1787/9789264222311-en.

OECD and the International Bank for Reconstruction and Development/The World Bank (2011), *Tracking Anti-Corruption and Asset Recovery Commitments. A Progress Report and Recommendations for Action*, OECD and the International Bank for Reconstruction and Development/The World Bank, Paris, www.oecd.org/dac/accountable-effective-institutions/Tracking%20Anti-corruption%20.pdf.

Chapter 2.

West Africa: Regional context and susceptibility to criminal economies

This chapter reviews the key characteristics of the West African region that are relevant both to understanding the growth of criminal economies, and their interactions with citizens and the state. These issues include the development and demographic status of West African countries, and the dynamics of the region's economy and trade. The chapter provides an overview of the region's governance and democracy, and highlights salient features of its peace and security, or instability. Taken together, these characteristics impact on the way criminality develops in the region. Consequently, they are relevant for developing responses to criminality and illicit financial flows, and working to mitigate the impact of these factors on development.

Introduction

This report focuses on West Africa and the 15 countries covered by the Economic Community of West African States (ECOWAS): Benin, Burkina Faso, Cabo Verde, Côte d'Ivoire, Gambia, Ghana, Guinea, Guinea-Bissau, Liberia, Mali, Niger, Nigeria, Senegal, Sierra Leone and Togo. ECOWAS brings these countries together around the shared commitment to build a "borderless, peaceful, prosperous and cohesive region, built on good governance" (ECOWAS, 2011). This commitment recognises that owing to a range of systemic factors, West African nations and peoples are uniquely bound together, with highly homogenous societies and interwoven, complementary economies. As borders between these states are highly porous, freedom of movement and trade sits at the cornerstone of a shared understanding of resilience, economic growth and development.

This section identifies some of the factors that make West African countries more susceptible to the impacts of illicit financial flows (IFFs) and criminal economies. While analysing the region as a whole, it recognises that West African countries are not uniform. They present appreciable differences in their forms of political institutionalisation, governance, economic performance and statebuilding, resulting in different political arrangements, institutions and patterns of economic development. These differences have affected the extent to which criminal economies and IFFs feature in the economy and infiltrate the state (Felbab-Brown, 2010). Arguably, governments' resilience and capacity to counter criminal economies and prevent IFFs reflect the resources available to them and their political will – thus making West African countries highly susceptible to the development of criminal economies and their resultant IFFs.

Though it is not possible to isolate the specific conditions that directly lead to criminal activity, certain structural factors appear to contribute to a country's vulnerability. These include "high unemployment, high income inequality, prior exposure to violence, democratic collapse, low gross domestic product and weak institutional capacity" (Cockayne, 2011), as well as the size of the informal economy compared to the formal economy. Combined with global dynamics, these factors highlight vulnerabilities to criminal activity and serve as bulwarks against effective responses.

This chapter reviews key characteristics of the region, relevant for understanding both the growth of criminal economies, and their interactions with citizens and the state. These will have consequences on the responses to criminality and IFFs arising in this context, as well as for those working to mitigate their impact on development.

Development and demographics

Compared with the high growth rates achieved between 2000 and 2010, the rate of human progress in African countries has declined in recent years. This decline is a reflection of the slowdown of increases in per-capita income relative to improvements in education and health outcomes. This slowdown is a concern, as most African countries still remain in the low human-development category. West Africa faces significant challenges in this area (African Development Bank [AfDB]/OECD/United Nations Development Programme [UNDP], 2016): 11 out of the 15 ECOWAS countries are Least developed countries (United Nations, 2016) and all of them – save two (Ghana and Cabo Verde) – remain in the bottom quartile of the United Nations Human Development Index (HDI) (Table 2.1).

Table 2.1. **Human development index ranking in 2016 (out of 187)**

ECOWAS state	HDI value
Benin	167
Burkina Faso	185
Cabo Verde	122
Côte d'Ivoire	171
Gambia	173
Ghana	139
Guinea	183
Guinea-Bissau	178
Liberia	177
Mali	175
Niger	187
Nigeria	152
Senegal	162
Sierra Leone	179
Togo	166

Source: UNDP (2016).

Owing to the topological conditions of the Sahara and Sahel, resilience systems in West Africa are unique. These systems have required a degree of mobility and inter-dependence among communities that belies the region's geographical distances and topography. Agricultural lands are scarce and thinly distributed. Whereas agro-pastoral production drives the economy in most of sub-Saharan Africa, in West Africa – and particularly in the Sahel – trade is the economic cornerstone, and seasonal exchange or travel are often the only options available (Krätli, Swift and Powell, 2014; OECD/Sahel and West Africa Club Secretariat [SWAC], 2014). Many analysts believe the populations of West Africa are better understood as a network that spans the Sahara, rather than as nation-states and borders (Meagher, 2005; Scheele, 2012; OECD/SWAC, 2014).

With low levels of agricultural production in rural areas, West Africa's development has been characterised by rapid urbanisation. In 1950, the region comprised 152 cities and major towns; today, it has nearly 2 000 – more than 12 times that number. In 1950, no urban area had a population of more than 1 million; now 22 such areas exist (OECD/SWAC, 2015). Urbanisation has profoundly shaped the region's economic, political and social environment (OECD/SWAC, 2014). State institutions are struggling to manage urban development effectively, leading to growing informal economies and settlements, and chronically poor living conditions for large portions of the population (AfDB, 2012).

Another defining feature of West Africa is its demographic profile. Where the population of continental Africa as a whole is young and growing at twice the pace of other continents', growth in West Africa is even more marked. Between 1950 and 2007, the region's population increased fourfold, from approximately 70 million to more than 300 million; 60% of the population is under 25 years of age, and one third is aged 15-24 years (Figure 2.1). This youth bulge is expected to plateau around 2050, at which point the region's population may have doubled, reaching 700 million people (Fortune et al., 2015).

This exponential population growth is a challenge for the effective delivery of services and realisation of development, even when growth is positive. For example, positive economic growth, regional integration and coherence have meant that ECOWAS has increased per-capita food production by more than 40% since the 1980s. Ensuring food security and creating productive livelihoods, however, remains a serious challenge: an estimated 36 million West Africans are still undernourished, and several million face food emergencies every year (FAOSTAT, 2015). Development in the health and education sector is challenged to provide the desired returns to meet the needs of growing populations.

Unemployment rates are high, particularly for youth. Improvements in technology and communication, and investments in education, have transformed young people's expectations with regard to employment and the future, yet these are out of step with opportunities in the formal sector, particularly for those completing higher education (Fortune et al., 2015; Marc et al., 2015; WA-IOM-130515). Economies have remained caught in predominantly informal, subsistence and basic trading activities. Limited high value-added work (AfDB, 2012) fails to offer most citizens any hope of social advancement or return on educational investment.

Informal enterprise accounts for anywhere between 40% and 75% of gross domestic product (GDP) and employs anywhere between 50% and 80% of the available workforce in different West African countries. By one estimate, the informal sector currently accounts for around 60% of all urban employment and provided 90% of all new employment created in the 1990s (Fortune et al., 2015). Consequently, economic growth has translated into increasing inequalities, and a highly visible gap between the "haves" and the "have nots". This, in turn, has caused young people to become disillusioned with their governments and has entrenched intergenerational differences (Reitman and Shaw, 2014; Marc et al., 2015). Arguably, these schisms have exacerbated social fractures and weakened the rule of law, with implications for the recruitment of youth into criminal industries.

Figure 2.1.**Evolution of ECOWAS countries' populations in millions, 1960-2030 (projected)**

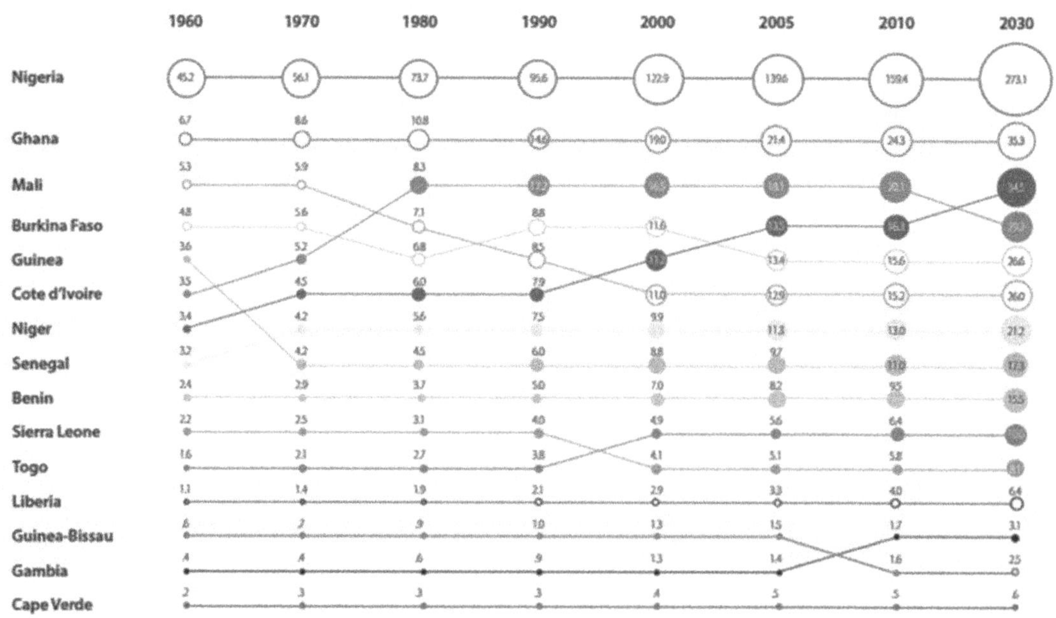

Note: Data are presented to indicate relative population size over time.

Sources: World Bank data (1960-2010); Population Pyramids of the World (2030).

Economy and trade

Like the rest of the world, West Africa has seen a surge in global trade flows over the last decade, mostly driven by natural-resource extraction. West Africa's proportional contribution to global imports and exports appears to be falling (UNCTAD, 2013), while the rest of Africa' share has remained constant or increased. Illicit activity, criminal economies and the diversion of legitimate trade flows outside of the formal economy could explain West Africa's relatively poor performance.

The establishment of ECOWAS in 1975 created a free-trade area. This was followed in 1994 by the creation of the West African Economic and Monetary Union (also known as Union Économique et Monétaire Ouest Africaine [UEMOA]). Eight countries within the UEMOA (Benin, Burkina Faso, Côte d'Ivoire, Guinea-Bissau, Mali, Niger, Senegal and Togo) share a common currency (the West African CFA franc), as well as common customs capacity. In terms of economic structure, UEMOA countries are heterogeneous. Although most depend on agriculture, services, and oil and mineral extraction as their primary economic drivers, only a few member countries have developed sizeable manufacturing industries. Mali, Niger and Burkina Faso are landlocked, while all other member countries have access to the sea. Cabo Verde – a small-island economy – has the highest GDP per capita, although Nigeria has by far the largest economy overall. The economies of ECOWAS countries have been growing quickly in the last 50 years. As Figure 2.2 shows, GDP grew from USD 50 billion to nearly USD 300 billion in real terms between 1966 and 2014, while the region as a whole achieved 4-5% growth rates per year over the same period (World Bank, 2014).

Figure 2.2.**GDP adjusted for inflation (2010) for ECOWAS states**

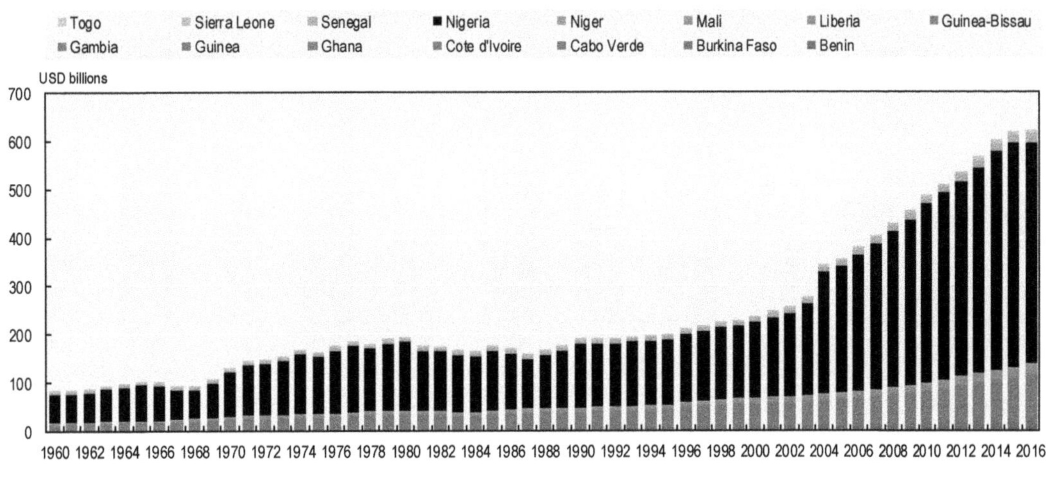

Source: World Bank (2017a).

Connections to the hydrocarbon-dominant economies of North Africa and the Maghreb have a significant impact on economic realities, as they create economic opportunities for goods, services, income and employment. For centuries, North African ports were global trade gateways to the Sahel countries and countries further south, with trade routes facilitated by nomadic groups spanning the Sahara. This northward pull was reinforced by the discovery of vast hydrocarbon reservoirs in Algeria and Libya; their boom economies and need for labour pushed the migration patterns from all the countries of sub-Saharan Africa northwards (OECD/SWAC, 2014).

The major evolution in trade patterns is relatively recent. Since 2009, over 90% of global trade has been moved by sea, 70% of it as container-based cargo. Significant investment in port infrastructure has considerably eased the region's integration into global trade. Key ports have become strategic points controlling the bulk of trade in the region (Harding, Pálsson and Raballand, 2007). This makes it easier and cheaper to extract natural resources from the mineral-rich Mano River and West African coastal regions, which boast plentiful deposits of base metals and precious metals, minerals and phosphates, as well as flora and fauna (OECD/SWAC, 2014). In the last decade, this global trend has triggered a rise in the volume of trade through West Africa, largely driven by the growth in demand from Asia (AfDB, 2010).

As Figure 2.3 shows, most trade for ECOWAS countries takes place outside of the region (Uexkull, 2012). The European Union has traditionally been the primary trading partner with West Africa, both for imports and exports. Côte d'Ivoire, Ghana and Nigeria account for 80% of West Africa's exports – mainly comprising fuel and food products – to the European Union. West Africa's imports from the European Union consist of fuels, food products, machinery, chemicals and pharmaceutical products (European Commission, 2015). In February 2014, the European Union and ECOWAS signed a new Economic Partnership Agreement that would grant West African states long-term access to the European market without being subjected to tariffs or quotas (European Commission, 2014).

Figure 2.3**Total goods: Export and import flows between Europe and West Africa**

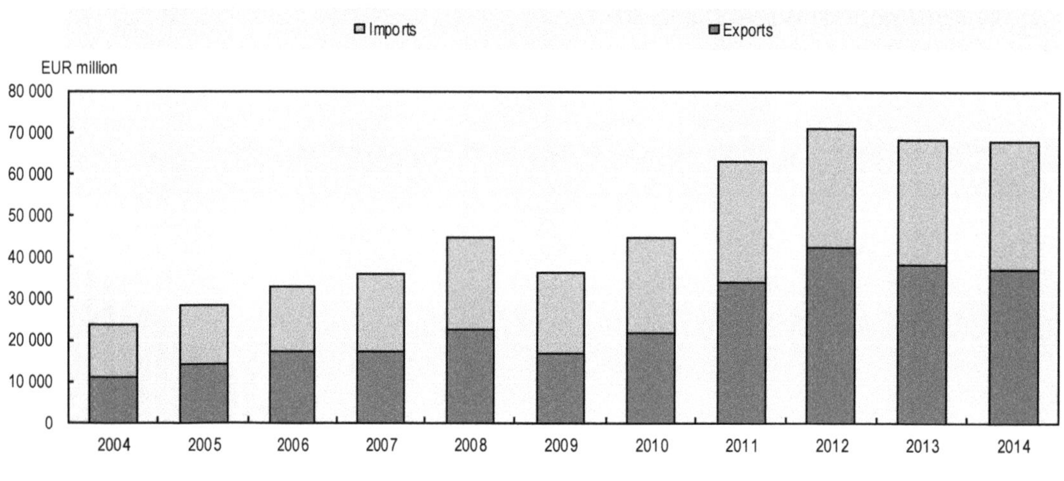

Source: ComSTAT (2015).

Over the past decade, Chinese exports to ECOWAS countries have expanded more than tenfold. The People's Republic of China (hereafter China) is now the largest national exporter to ECOWAS (Figure 2.4). In Ghana, for example, imports from China account for around 20% of total imports.

The bulk of counterfeit and substandard goods brought into West Africa is concealed within legitimate trade flows into the region. Limited state resources, endemic corruption within port authorities and a lack of capacity to physically inspect most containers provide an environment conducive to contraband shipments. Control of imports and product quality in the marketplace is also limited.

From a global perspective, West Africa remains a relatively small market and a relatively complex operating environment. OECD estimates of the prevalence of counterfeit goods based on customs-seizure data suggest a global increase, but no reliable regional figures exist. Anecdotally, the perception is that both substandard and counterfeit goods are highly prevalent in West Africa, and that the problem has grown.

The seizure data indicate that China is the main source country of fake and counterfeit goods (including foodstuffs, pharmaceuticals, and a wide variety of consumer and fake luxury goods) heading to West Africa and the United Arab Emirates. China serve as transit points to West African markets. West African countries have also served as transit points to other countries on the continent (OECD/European Union Intellectual Property Office, 2017).

Figure 2.4.**Top ten (non-ECOWAS) import partners for all ECOWAS countries combined, 2003-15**

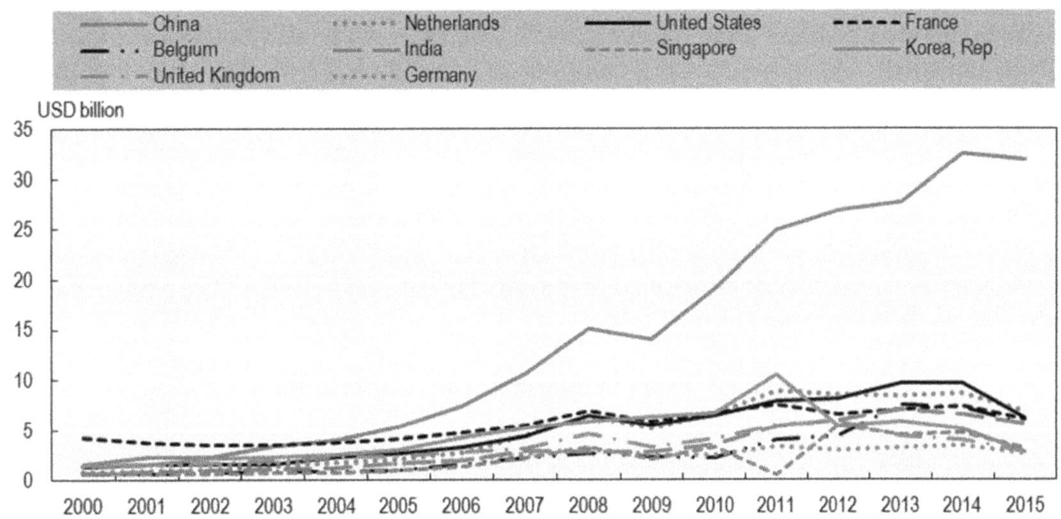

Source: OECD Development Centre; calculations based on *UN Comtrade database* (2017).

With their economies so heavily driven by external exports, the ability of regional governments to fund development strategies depends on their capacity to capture a fair share of the export wealth generated by minerals and other resources. In the report *Track it! Stop it! Get it! Illicit Financial Flows from Africa*, the High Level Panel (HLP) on Illicit Financial Flows from Africa made three key points: African governments are unable or unwilling to successfully negotiate resource-extraction contracts that are fair and favourable in the long term; private companies investing in the region combine legal, illegal and borderline activities to limit taxation; and the international financial system provides loopholes and jurisdictions in which capital resources and revenues can be diverted (United Nations Economic Commission for Africa [ECA]/HLP, 2015).

The Africa Progress Panel (2013) has suggested that African governments lack the resources necessary to effectively assess the tax liabilities of overseas organisations. As a result, these organisations may be able to engage in tax evasion or aggressive tax avoidance. When countries have attempted to reform the taxation system against the interests of powerful corporations, these corporations have used their position to rail against such moves (ECA, 2011). Tax is also evaded through misinvoicing, typically for intangible goods or services (e.g. intergroup loans, intellectual-property taxes, procurement costs, and expert or management fees). Misinvoicing practices have been used in multiple ways, e.g. to pay bribes and reduce profit margins (ECA/HLP, 2015).

Trade within the ECOWAS zone is limited, with 10-15% of total exports going to regional markets. From 2015, ECOWAS adopted common tariffs against the outside world, and established a customs union featuring free trade between the member states and a common trade policy that overrides national law. The common external tariff for consumer goods is set at 20%; the external tariff for specific goods boosting economic development is set at 30%. Individual member states do, however, maintain the option to institute import bans and quotas, and to set taxes. Hence, the customs union is still not fully realised (International Centre for Trade and Sustainable Development, 2015).

All countries in the region have sizeable informal economies. An estimated 40-80% of economic activity takes place outside of the formal banking sector. In 2012, the ECA argued that informal cross-border trade constituted on average 43% of GDP; case studies in West Africa and the Horn of Africa show that informal cross-border trade vastly exceeds reported bilateral trade (Golub, 2015). The ECA study also noted that in some – albeit unnamed – African countries, informal regional trade flows may constitute up to 90% of official trade movement (ECA, 2012).

The ECA defines informal cross-border trade as the movement of legitimately produced goods and services that avoid custom controls and/or pass through official channels. They use illegal practices such as under-invoicing (reporting a lower quantity, weight or value of goods to incur lower tariffs) and misclassification (falsifying the description of goods so they appear to be goods attracting a lower tariff). The ECA posited three categories of informal cross-border trade (Table 2.2).

Table 2.2. **Types of informal cross-border trade**

Category A	Category B	Category C
Informal (unregistered) traders or firms operating entirely outside the formal economy	Formal (registered) firms fully evading trade-related regulations and duties (e.g. avoiding official border-crossing posts)	Formal (registered) firms partially evading trade-related regulations and duties by resorting to illegal practices (e.g. under-invoicing)

Source: ECA (2012).

Continually fragmented policies on taxation, quotas, tariffs and currency control have meant that cross-border illicit trade has flourished within the ECOWAS zone. Mbaye (2014) argued that in West Africa, "… documented intra-regional trade is small but smuggling is pervasive, despite regional integration schemes intended to promote official trade." The assessment further argued that "[c]ross border trade involves a complex interplay of formal and informal operators and practices" and "[e]thnic and religious networks play a large role in organizing the informal sector, resulting in a set of shadow institutions that in some respects are more effective and powerful than official institutions" (Mbaye, 2014).

Informal trade of this sort, however, should be distinguished from criminal cross-border trafficking. Faleye (2014) asserts that "there is clear distinction between criminals involved in the trafficking of illegal goods, such as guns, which are a direct threat to national security and informal cross-border traders who buy and sell 'legal goods' including contraband commodity goods, such as clothes, which contribute to the wellbeing of the masses of the society."

For example, one of the most significant border regions in West Africa lies between Nigeria and Benin. The economies of these two countries rely upon both illegal and legal cross-border trade, "an essential part of the Abidjan-Lagos transport and migration corridor", which "also represents a key transport vein in the ECOWAS region" (Blum, 2014). A similar narrative applies to the Saharan states bordering North Africa, where variable pastoral conditions, minimal domestic resources or industries, and heavily subsidised commodities in the oil-rich states of North Africa contribute to highly mobile populations and active cross-border trading networks. With 16 794 kilometres of land borders between the Sahel states, Algeria and Libya, cross-border trade in subsidised commodities is significant (OECD/SWAC, 2014). Research has shown that Algeria provides transport subsidies in the range of USD 12.5 million per year to ensure that subsidised commodities reach communities in the country's southern regions. This has created a cross-border smuggling economy, estimated at around USD 50 million with communities in northern Mali. The fiscal cost of food and energy subsidies from the government of Libya before the current crisis amounted to USD 11.5 billion a year (equivalent to nearly 14% of Libya's GDP); smuggling of licit commodities from Libya alone has been estimated at USD 4 billion per year (Reitano and Shaw, 2014).

In the Sahel and West Africa, active networks of informal cross-border trade have facilitated the growth of more damaging criminal cross-border trafficking. Local border populations – who depend on, protect and sustain smuggling networks – do not distinguish between commodities with varying degrees of illegality (OECD/SWAC, 2014). This has implications for those seeking to combat illicit trade. Strengthening lengthy and porous borders requires overcoming the entrenched nature and legitimacy of cross-border informal trade, and accounting for the livelihoods associated with it. Most of the goods available in this region are smuggled commodities; in fact, the communities provide services for traffickers. Successful smugglers and traffickers are seldom stigmatised, and may be lauded by communities where informal trade is the rule, rather than the exception (OECD/SWAC, 2014; Reitano and Shaw, 2014). As seaborne trade has increasingly superseded the need for land-based trade, smuggling and trafficking of increasingly high-value illicit commodities have penetrated the informal economy. Some analysts have argued that the distinction between informal and formal economies is less valid, and that the economy should instead be understood as a series of social networks based around kith and kin (Meagher, 2005).

Most transactions in the informal economy – including those supporting illegal activities – are paid in cash or through informal financing mechanisms. Financial services in the ECOWAS region are available to a small segment of the population: access to finance averages only 20%, ranging from 6% in Sierra Leone to 51% of the adult population in Cabo Verde (Inter-Governmental Action Group against Money Laundering in West Africa [GIABA], 2014a). Similarly, a large proportion of remittances – which are among the largest contributors to domestic income in most West African economies – travel outside of the formal banking system. For example, surveys in Burkina Faso and Senegal revealed that over 60% of the receiving households used informal channels for cross-border remittances (World Bank, 2011), affecting the capacity of the region's governments to benefit from taxation. At the same time, senders are paying a disproportionate cost for their transactions, owing to two major challenges: the high rates of informality (particularly within the continent) and a regulatory environment favouring monopolies.

Most African countries restrict outbound flows of money, unless they are used for trade or being deposited in banking institutions (International Fund for Agricultural Development, n.d.). In West Africa, a single money transfer operator (MTO) handles 70% of official payments. It also has a monopoly on money transfers between banks

(Watkins and Quattri, 2014). In Nigeria, a single MTO handles nearly 80% of remittance transfers, valued in excess of USD 20.5 billion per year; it also expects exclusivity and prevents other MTOs from entering into agreements with banks disbursing remittances. Since banks are the only entities allowed to receive and distribute money transfers, a small group of financial institutions end up handling all official flows, relying on fewer than four MTOs (International Fund for Agricultural Development, n.d.).

As a result, the costs of transactions between the formal and the informal economy are high, and borne by those who are least able to absorb them. Members of Africa's diaspora pay a 12% fee to send USD 200; that is almost double the global average, and significantly higher than the pledge made by United Nations (UN) member states in the context of the 2030 Agenda for Sustainable Development to bring the cost down to 3% (United Nations, 2015). In effect, it means that Africans are paying a "super tax" on their remittances. Moreover, despite the principles of free movement of goods and people, and the creation of ECOWAS as a free-trade zone, transactions within West Africa itself incur some of the highest charge structures in the world. A study by Watkins and Quattri (2014) found that migrant Ghanaian workers remitting money from Nigeria can face charges well above 20%; this is a significant disincentive to regional trade and transactions. Converting that gap into financial terms, the study estimated that Africa is losing between USD 1.4 billion and USD 2.3 billion per year as a result of high remittance charges.

Various informal solutions have emerged to meet the needs of migrants and communities stemming from strong regulation in the formal economy and barriers to entry. Operating outside of the formal financial sector, *hawala*[1] dealers provide money-transfer systems using trust-based networks of cash exchange. While this has proven to be an effective low-cost solution, the risks are relatively high that these systems will be used for transfers related to criminal activity (e.g. drug trafficking, human trafficking and money laundering) or terrorist financing (Financial Action Task Force [FATF], 2015; SEN-GIABA-130515; UK-Gov-LE-220615). Moreover, they further exclude large segments of West African populations from the formal banking sector (OECD, 2014), particularly as the threats of terrorist financing raise the level of external regulation.

Governance and democracy

The 2014 West Africa Commission on Drugs (WACD) determined that corruption at the top is facilitating drug trafficking across the subcontinent. It found that traffickers were able to connect easily with people of influence by both creating and using informal social networks to access or co-opt the formal security apparatus where necessary. One key weakness (though by no means restricted to West Africa) appears to be the electoral process. Most African nations have limited or no restrictions on campaign funding and do not possess monitoring mechanisms, making them susceptible to offers of illicit resources (WACD, 2014). Once elected, politicians distribute access to resources based on patronage, rather than development objectives. In certain countries, the levels of capital flight (both from illicit and legitimate resources) are significant.

West African states feature some of the weakest governance indicators in the world. As Table 2.3 shows, most score in the bottom quartile for key indicators such as rule of law, government effectiveness, political stability, accountability and control over corruption (Kaufmann, Kraay and Maastruzzi, 2015). In addition to – or interconnected with – the low governance indicators, ECOWAS states are also marred by high levels of corruption. Numerous studies (both quantitative and perception-based) have found corruption in almost all facets of private and public life. Ghana was the highest performer on

Transparency International's Transparency Corruption Perceptions Index: it ranked as the eighth least-corrupt country in sub-Saharan Africa – higher than South Africa – but still scored less than one-half of 100 possible points. Nigeria, the region's largest economy, ranked close to the bottom: it was assessed as the 136th least-corrupt country, scoring only one-quarter of the maximum possible points. The Ibrahim Index on African Governance (IIAG) shows that while most countries in Africa score less than 40% for accountability, the indicators for two-thirds of ECOWAS countries are worsening, rather than improving (IIAG, 2014). Citizens experience corruption on all scales: small-scale graft by local officials is almost an alternative form of taxation on the most common forms of civic engagement, such as registering births or deaths, obtaining identification and conducting business (Reitano and Shaw, 2014). At a higher level, the state diverts resources.

Table 2.3. **ECOWAS states ranked according to various indices**

ECOWAS member state	World Governance Indicators (percentile ranks 0 to 100)						Corruption Perception Index		Mo Ibrahim Index	Press freedom
	Voice and accountability	Political stability	Government effectiveness	Regulatory quality	Rule of law	Control of corruption	Rank	Score	(out of 100 countries)	
Benin	63	48	33	30	29	36	95	36	57.5	30.32
Burkina Faso	48	15	34	37	34	53	72	42	51.8	23.85
Cabo Verde	78	77	56	42	63	79	38	59	73	18.02
Côte d'Ivoire	36	16	26	39	28	33	108	34	52.3	30.42
Gambia	13	27	19	31	25	22	145	26	46.6	46.7
Ghana	67	40	46	45	54	50	70	43	63.9	17.95
Guinea	26	30	14	19	8	14	142	27	43.3	33.15
Guinea-Bissau	27	28	4	8	6	3	168	16	41.3	30.09
Liberia	43	25	8	15	17	26	90	37	50	31.12
Mali	39	8	15	28	22	29	116	32	50.6	38.27
Niger	34	11	31	26	29	31	101	35	50.2	27.21
Nigeria	35	6	12	18	13	13	136	28	46.5	39.69
Senegal	57	36	36	49	47	57	64	45	60.8	26.72
Sierra Leone	42	40	10	16	21	20	123	30	49.4	30.73
Togo	32	38	12	22	27	28	116	32	48.5	30.75

Notes: The Worldwide Governance Indicators are a dataset summarising the views of a large number of enterprise, citizen and expert survey respondents in industrial and developing countries on the quality of governance in their country. The higher the percentage score, the higher the subjective assessment of the quality of governance.

The Corruption Perception Index ranks countries and territories based on the perceptions of corruption in the public sector. A country or territory's score indicates the perceived level of public-sector corruption on a scale of 0 (highly corrupt) to 100 (very clean).

The Ibrahim Index of African Governance (IIAG) measures the quality of governance in every African country on an annual basis. Data are compiled along four overarching dimensions, with constituent subcategories covering a total of 93 indicators from 33 data providers. These are added to provide a score out of 100.

The Reporters Without Borders Press Freedom Index combines qualitative assessments based on a survey submitted to journalists, researchers, jurists and human-rights defenders in 180 countries covered by the Index. The survey is complemented by quantitative criteria based on monitoring work done by Reporters Without Borders. The Index aims to measure the level of violence and harassment inflicted on journalists and other information providers during the period. Scores range from 0-100, with 0 being the best possible score, and 100 being the worst.

Sources: World Bank (2017b); Transparency International (2016); Mo Ibrahim Foundation (2016); Reporters Without Borders (2016).

While the transition from authoritarianism to more open multi-party democracies across the region has been a positive development, it has challenged the integrity of the electoral process and increased the region's susceptibility to illicit flows. Elections are not publicly funded in West Africa, and many candidates own their parties. They fund their campaigns through private resources or raise support from friends, regional allies or their ethnic base. This reinforces clientelism and patronage in the political system. It also renders West Africa's electoral processes vulnerable to corruption by criminal actors, or donors to political parties or electoral campaigns who are keen to ensure favourable conditions (WACD, 2014). The 2011 Praia Declaration on Elections and Stability in West Africa, signed by all leaders in the ECOWAS region, recognised this fact. Most of its recommendations and provisions, however, have not been implemented.

Illicit trafficking routes in West Africa have also proven to be a lucrative avenue for governments and officials to top up their funds, particularly in those countries without significant natural-resource wealth. Smuggling is widely tolerated, and law enforcement is fitful and inefficient (United Nations Office on Drugs and Crime [UNODC], 2013). A growing body of evidence shows that members of organised-crime syndicates have infiltrated politics and economies in West Africa.

Participation in trafficking appears to offer political, military and business leaders windfall profits: they can conduct electoral and military campaigns, feed patronage systems, or simply take a fast track to wealth and power. In turn, politicians and security leaders can offer traffickers protection, or even assistance. The pattern is clearest in Guinea-Bissau. After the December 2008 coup in Guinea, Latin American cocaine traders reportedly moved to the country (as well as to Burkina Faso and Benin) in significant numbers, reproducing the pattern of collusion (UNODC, 2013). Thus, one of the principal – and most damaging – features of illicit financial flows in West Africa is arguably the way criminal organisations are mirroring the existing networks of licit power, exploiting advantageous positions close to official power to gain benefits and opportunities for illicit activities (Goudsmid, Mancini and Vanegas Canosa, 2012; WA-CivSoc-130515).

The governance of resource wealth and development presents another important disconnect. Resource-rich countries have largely failed to use resource revenue to support development strategies or establish production linkages with the rest of the economy. As former UN Secretary-General Kofi Annan stated in his concluding remarks at the 2013 Africa Progress Panel:

> Africa's resource wealth has bypassed the vast majority of African people and built vast fortunes for a privileged few. Mineral exports have financed monuments in Europe, generated profits for foreign investors, and benefitted commercial and political elites. Few African countries have successfully used their natural-resource capital to extend opportunity, combat poverty and support dynamic, inclusive growth. (Africa Progress Panel, 2013)

Among all the countries in the West African region, Nigeria stands out. Despite its extraordinary financial resources, derived from the oil industry, the country remains the largest driver of IFFs. It is a large recipient of official development assistance, and yet poverty and development indicators remain low. Governments have failed to take systematic measures to counter oil theft or reduce state protection of this illicit trade, and this has fuelled a range of criminal economies, both within the country and in the region, including growing maritime piracy, kidnapping for ransom and trafficking in a range of commodities.

Worldwide, changes in government – whether unconstitutional or constitutional, violent or non-violent – present both an opportunity and a threat to the quality of governance and the integration of criminal actors into the democratic process. In West Africa, governments in the immediate post-conflict period have proven vulnerable to poor decisions associated with mining concessions and other trade policies: typically, the economy has been disrupted, driving an urgent need for liquid resources. Owing to financing restrictions, development assistance may have been suspended, exacerbating this need (Mailey, 2015).

Hundreds of millions of dollars in assets of leaders have been frozen pending investigation under initiatives like the Kleptocrat Asset Recovery Initiative, spearheaded by the United States. These investigations into finances held in foreign jurisdictions provide some insight into how much money is being stolen. Transparent national investigations or reports – such as the report by Audit Service Sierra Leone (2014), which suggested that some 30% of funds earmarked for Sierra Leone's Ebola expenditure were unaccounted for – are the exception.

The impact of elite impunity, coupled with widespread corruption, is citizen disenfranchisement, underinvestment in development and political instability. This effect is prevalent in all countries, but is most acute in resource-rich nations, where obvious resources exist, but other priorities divert or crowd out development-oriented public spending. Poorly targeted food and fuel subsidies benefit the non-poor more than their intended beneficiaries. Revenue-sharing arrangements – where they exist – seldom reflect national strategies for poverty reduction (Africa Progress Panel, 2013). Combined, these factors create states that are chronically lacking in global competitiveness (Table 2.4).

Table 2.4. **Performance on indicators of global competitiveness for some ECOWAS countries, 2015-16**

ECOWAS member state	Public trust in politicians		Irregular payments and bribes		Transparency of government policy making		Business cost of crime and violence		Organised crime	
	Score	Rank (out of 140)	Score	Rank (out of 140)	Score	Rank (out of 140)	Score	Rank (out of 140)	Score	Rank (out of 140)
Benin	3.0	63	2.4	13.5	3.6	110	4.6	70	4.4	92
Cabo Verde	3.4	48	4.2	54	4.1	67	4.0	100	4.5	88
Côte d'Ivoire	3.7	38	4.2	55	4.4	50	3.5	113	3.4	127
Gambia	3.8	36	4.1	59	4.5	38	5.4	33	5.8	28
Ghana	3.1	61	3.1	109	3.9	87	4.1	95	4.3	98
Guinea	2.3	104	2.1	138	3.0	132	3.6	112	4.1	106
Liberia	3.8	35	3.7	80	3.8	93	4.3	84	4.4	91
Mali	3.3	52	2.8	126	3.8	94	3.4	117	3.6	123
Nigeria	1.7	132	2.6	132	3.4	121	3.1	125	4.1	109
Senegal	3.2	57	3.6	91	4.2	59	4.7	64	4.8	73
Sierra Leone	2.5	96	2.3	13	3.6	109	3.8	105	4.1	108

Note: Score is calculated as per-country compliance against a series of pre-established indicators. Score is the country's ranking against the 140 countries compared in the report.

Source: World Economic Forum (2014).

The international community plays an important role in signalling acceptable governance standards, and placing bulwarks between criminal associations and governance. The decision to legitimise (or not) an unconstitutional change in government sends an important signal.

Peace and security

Fragility, insecurity and conflict, as well as growing violent extremism, undermine state institutions, set back development progresses and facilitate the growth of criminal economies in the region. Most West African states gained their independence between 1960 and 1975. Since then, a number of protracted, violent conflicts have beset the region, with countries experiencing at least 60 coups and attempted coups, as well as numerous civil wars and insurgencies. Armed rebel and terrorist groups – often enriched by illicit resources – remain active across the region. With the high prevalence of weapons in circulation, used in everything from insurgencies and criminal protection to electoral violence, these threats are proving increasingly difficult to quell.

In the last decade, the nature of conflict in the region has changed. It has evolved from civil wars towards lower level, protracted insurgencies predicated on ethnic or nationalistic grievances, including repeated acts of terrorism against both domestic and foreign targets (Table 2.5).

Table 2.5. **Selected conflicts in West Africa**

Name of conflict	Country	Years	Nature of conflict	Estimated fatalities
Guinea-Bissau War of Independence	Guinea-Bissau	1962-74	Insurgency	15 000
Biafran War	Nigeria	1967-70	Civil war	500 000-2 000 000
Casamance conflict	Senegal	1982-present	Insurgency	5 000
First Liberian Civil War	Liberia	1989-96	Civil war	100 000-220 000
First Tuareg Rebellion	Mali	1990-95	Insurgency	–
Sierra Leone Civil War	Sierra Leone	1991-2002	Civil war	50 000-300 000
Guinea-Bissau Civil War	Guinea-Bissau	1998-99	Civil war	655
Second Liberian Civil War	Liberia	1999-2003	Civil war	150 000-300 000
First Ivorian Civil War	Côte d'Ivoire	2002-07	Civil war	3 000
Niger Delta Conflict	Nigeria	2004-09	Insurgency	2 500-4 000
Second Tuareg Rebellion	Niger	2007-09	Insurgency	270-400
Boko Haram uprising	Nigeria	2009 – present	Insurgency	11 200
Second Ivorian Civil War	Côte d'Ivoire	2010-11	Civil war	3 000
Conflict in Northern Mali	Mali	2012-13	Insurgency	1 270

Source: Marc et al. (2015).

Marc et al. (2015) identify five major conflict systems in West Africa (Figure 2.5) that engage in repeated cycles of violence. Although conflicts may have an epicentre, the systemic features of the region's geography and demography, and the societal structure of West African populations, mean that a conflict rarely stays contained. Porous borders, and geographically dispersed and highly mobile populations, increase the chances of negative spillovers, either through movements of arms, combatants or people displaced by conflict. Many conflict systems have long trajectories, with cyclical flare-ups of violence over decades.

The Mali crisis, and the resulting fragmentation and dispersion of insurgent groups, have increased the challenge of effectively tackling conflict and violence in the West African region. Individual membership in conflict groups changes with circumstances, although it generally continues to align with tribal or ethnic cleavages (OECD/SWAC, 2014). Conflict zones have widened beyond their typical sites of concentration, and there is increasing evidence that groups are learning from each other. For example, groups in the Sahel affiliated with Al-Qaeda in the Islamic Maghreb have provided training, financing and support to Boko Haram in Nigeria. At the same time, the proliferating groups in the Sahel have been copying Boko Haram's financing and attack methods (Reitano, Knoope and Oustinoff, 2016; NE-Gov-LE- 220915).

The shift from interstate conflict to violent extremism, exemplified by the sharp rise in terrorist incidents, is worrying (Figure 2.6). While incidents related to Boko Haram in Nigeria largely drive this trend, Mali and the Sahel face similar challenges. The presence of significant criminal economies both fuels terrorism, and provides justification for the further solicitation of illicit resources and engagement in criminal practices. Thus, while organised crime and terror actors are distinct, their goals and objectives have become mutually reinforcing.

Figure 2.5. **Conflict systems in West Africa**

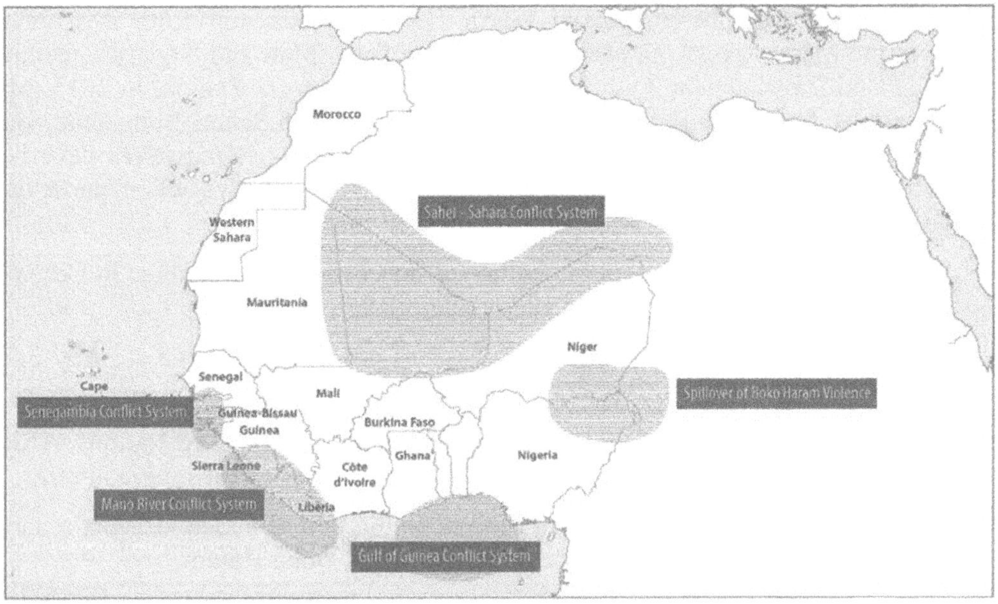

Source: Marc et al. (2015), with modifications by the authors.

Figure 2.6. **Terrorism incidents, 2000-16**

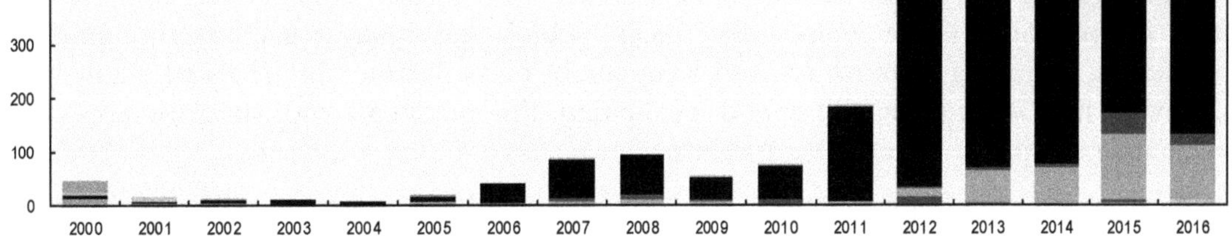

Source: START (2017).

International co-operation and regional co-ordination

As observed, regional integration is a fundamental concept in West Africa, given the interdependence and heterogeneity of its people. A number of overlapping regional co-ordination mechanisms address different aspects of political, economic, social and security priorities. The desire to counter the growth of illicit trafficking and terrorism in West Africa seems to have motivated further regional co-operation, both within West Africa and with its immediate neighbours.

All West African nations are members of the African Union. Of the 15 ECOWAS states, 14 (all but Cabo Verde) are members of the Community of Sahel-Saharan States. Eight are UEMOA members. Liberia, Sierra Leone Guinea and Côte d'Ivoire are members of the Mano River Union. Finally, Burkina Faso, Mali and Niger are members of the Integrated Development Authority of the Liptako-Gourma Region. In 2015, Mali, Nigeria, Burkina Faso, Mauritania and Chad, created the G5 Sahel. Both under these various umbrellas and in addition to them, several new regional initiatives have been launched to respond to the need for closer co-ordination and collective action, particularly with regard to the high levels of cross-border insecurity. These include:

- the Global Alliance for Resilience Initiative, launched in Ouagadougou in December 2012
- the Nouakchott Process, launched in 2013 to promote collective security in the region under the African Union's auspices
- the Bamako ministerial platform, launched after the joint United Nations, African Union, World Bank and European Union high-level visit to the region in 2013
- the revitalisation of the Lake Chad Basin Commission, founded in 1964, to tackle common border issues in response to the growth of Boko Haram.

The growing alignment and co-operation among West African countries, as well as with their immediate neighbours, signals efforts to move towards a common understanding of the challenges facing the region and the need for collaboration. In some cases, this has translated into the creation of regional instruments, including high-level declarations and common strategies, legal frameworks, trade policies and other joint initiatives, to govern collective behaviour (Table 2.6).

The major global instruments in the fight against criminal economies and IFFs are the United Nations Convention against Transnational Organized Crime (UNTOC) and the United Nations Convention against Corruption (UNCAC), as well as the protocols against drug trafficking and terrorism. Most West African states are parties to the major conventions and international frameworks in these areas (Table 2.7).

A number of peer-reviewed international norms and standard-setting bodies complement these conventions. These include the FATF, which sets measures countering money laundering, financing of terrorism and weapons of mass destruction. The real challenge, however, lies in understanding and evaluating the practical implementation of the mechanisms required under these standards.

Peer reviews are in place to assess anti-money laundering/countering the financing of terrorism (AML/CFT) measures. Earlier round of evaluations conducted by a FATF-style regional body in West Africa (GIABA) covered the requirement that countries introduce legal and administrative frameworks to combat money laundering and terrorist financing, although they focused on technical compliance with the standards, and did not go into much detail on the implementation of those laws and processes. State compliance with the AML/CFT framework varies across the West African region. Nearly all states have legislation in place to address money laundering and terrorist financing (Table 2.8). To date, however, at least one-half of West African countries have struggled to fully comply with key FATF requirements. These include adequately criminalising money laundering

Table 2.6. **Selection of regional mechanisms to counter criminal economies and IFFs**

Regional body	Description	Membership	Date created
ECOWAS Convention on Extradition	The Convention stipulates the conditions under which criminals can be extradited between signatory countries.	Burkina Faso, Cabo Verde, Ghana, Guinea, Mali, Niger, Nigeria, Senegal, Sierra Leone and Togo	1994
ECOWAS Convention on Mutual Assistance in Criminal Matters	The Convention stipulates states parties' commitments to assist each other in criminal investigations and proceedings.	Burkina Faso, Cabo Verde, Gambia, Ghana, Guinea, Mali, Niger, Nigeria, Senegal, Sierra Leone and Togo	1998
Intergovernmental Action Group against Money Laundering in Africa (GIABA)	This is a specialised body to strengthen capacity of member states in preventing and controlling money laundering and terrorist financing.	ECOWAS plus Sao Tome and Principe	1999
ECOWAS Protocol Relating to the Mechanism for Conflict Prevention, Management, Resolution, Peace-keeping and Security	The Protocol creates a wide range of bodies, organs and instruments to prevent and end conflict. It states political positions and sets out areas for co-operation.	ECOWAS	1999
2008 ECOWAS Regional Action Plan, Political Declaration and Operational Plan against Illicit Drug Trafficking, Abuse and Organised Crimes	The Action Plan is a formal articulation of ECOWAS Member States' positions on drug trafficking and on several other crimes.	ECOWAS	2008
ECOWAS Committee of Chiefs of Security Services	The Committee of national gendarmerie commanders collaborates with INTERPOL, developing co-operation among regional security forces, and defining and implementing a strategy for cross-border crime.	ECOWAS	2009
West Africa Coast Initiative	The Initiative has significant international funding to tackle serious organised crime by setting up transnational crime units in West African states.	Côte d'Ivoire, Guinea-Bissau, Liberia and Sierra Leone	2009
Network of West African Central Authorities and Prosecutors against Organized Crime	The Network strengthens the capacity of central authorities and prosecutors to combat organised crime, as well as increases regional co-operation on criminal matters.	ECOWAS, plus Mauritania	2012

Source: Compilation by the authors.

and terrorism financing, and establishing customer due-diligence requirements for financial institutions, designated non-financial businesses and professionals. The FATF has placed only two countries from the region – Nigeria in 2001 and Ghana in 2012 – on a list of high-risk and non-cooperative jurisdictions. West African countries that present significant deficiencies may not be subject to intensive monitoring by the FATF owing to their small financial sectors. The GIABA evaluation praised West African states for "demonstrating a political commitment to improving AML/CFT systems", but acknowledged that terrorist financing and money laundering remain a huge problem (GIABA, 2010).

Table 2.7. **Status of ECOWAS countries in regard to relevant international conventions**

ECOWAS member state	States party to 1988 UN Drug Convention[1]	States party to International Terror Finance Convention[2]	States party to UNTOC	States party to UNCAC	States party to the Arms Trade Treaty
Benin	Y	Y	Y	Y	Y
Burkina Faso	Y	Y	Y	Y	Y
Cabo Verde	Y	Y	Y	Y	Y
Côte d'Ivoire	Y	Y	Y	Y	Y
Gambia	Y	Y	Y	Y	**N**
Ghana	Y	Y	Y	Y	Y
Guinea	Y	Y	Y	Y	Y
Guinea-Bissau	Y	Y	Y	Y	Y*
Liberia	Y	Y	Y	Y	Y
Mali	Y	Y	Y	Y	Y
Niger	Y	Y	Y	Y	Y
Nigeria	Y	Y	Y	Y	Y
Senegal	Y	Y	Y	Y	Y
Sierra Leone	Y	Y	Y	Y	Y
Togo	Y	Y	Y	Y	Y

1. United Nations Convention against Illicit Traffic in Narcotic Drugs and Psychotropic Substances, 1988.

2. International Convention for the Suppression of the Financing of Terrorism, 1999.

* Signed, but not ratified.

Notes: Y = Yes, N = No.

Table 2.8. **Legislation enacted to combat money laundering and terrorist financing**

ECOWAS Country	Criminalised drug money laundering	Criminalised money laundering beyond drugs	Know your customer Provisions	Report large transactions	Report suspicious transactions	Maintain records over time	Disclosure protection" safe harbour"	Criminalise" tipping off"	Cross-border transportation of currency	Financial Intelligence Unit	International law enforcement co-operation	System for identifying/forfeiting assets	Arrangements for asset sharing	Criminalised financing of terrorism	Report suspected terrorist financing	Ability to freeze terrorist assets without delay	US or international sanctions/penalties
Benin	Y	Y	Y	**N**	Y	Y	Y	Y	Y	Y*	Y	Y	**N**	**N**	Y	Y	**N**
Burkina Faso	Y	Y	Y	Y	Y	Y	Y	Y	**N**	Y	Y	**N**	**N**	Y	Y	**N**	**N**
Cabo Verde	Y	Y	Y	Y	Y	Y	Y	**N**	Y	Y*	Y	Y	**N**	Y	Y	**N**	**N**
Côte d'Ivoire	Y	Y	Y	Y	Y	Y	**N**	Y	Y	Y	Y	Y	**N**	Y	Y	Y	Y
Gambia	Y	Y	Y	Y	Y	Y	Y	Y	Y	Y*	Y	Y	**N**	Y	Y	Y	**N**
Ghana	Y	Y	Y	Y	Y	Y	Y	Y	Y	Y	Y	Y	**N**	Y	Y	Y	**N**
Guinea	Y	Y	Y	**N**	Y	Y	Y	Y	Y	**N**	Y	**N**	**N**	Y	**N**	**N**	**N**
Guinea- Bissau	Y	Y	Y	**N**	Y	Y	Y	**N**	**N**	Y*	Y	Y	Y	Y	**N**	**N**	Y
Liberia	Y	Y	Y	**N**	Y	Y	Y	Y	Y	Y*	Y	Y	**N**	Y	Y	**N**	**N**
Mali	Y	Y	Y	Y	Y	Y	Y	Y	Y	Y	Y	**N**	**N**	Y	Y	**N**	**N**
Niger	Y	Y	Y	**N**	Y	Y	**N**	Y	Y	Y*	Y	Y	**N**	Y	Y	**N**	**N**
Nigeria	Y	Y	Y	Y	Y	Y	**N**	Y	Y	Y	Y	Y	**N**	Y	Y	Y	**N**
Senegal	Y	Y	Y	**N**	Y	Y	Y	Y	Y	Y	Y	Y	Y	Y	Y	Y	**N**
Sierra Leone	Y	Y	Y	Y	Y	Y	Y	Y	Y	Y*	Y	Y	**N**	Y	Y	**N**	**N**
Togo	Y	Y	Y	**N**	Y	Y	Y	Y	Y	Y	Y	Y	**N**	Y	Y	Y	**N**

Notes: Y = Yes, N = No.

Financial Intelligence Unit: An asterisk (*) reflects those jurisdictions whose FIUs are not members of the Egmont Group of FIUs.

Source: US Department of State (2016).

Arguably, the success of any AML regime does not lie with the ratified conventions, but with its effectiveness. While ratification is relatively strong, the implementation of protocols – i.e. codifying them into law and putting them to use – faces greater challenges. Since 2013, the latest round of FATF assessments have focused on the effectiveness of a country's AML/CFT systems; they go beyond the existence of relevant legislation or procedures to determine whether they are being utilised in line with the money laundering/terrorist financing risks present in the country. This will provide a much clearer understanding of the real issues facing authorities in implementing effective measures to combat money laundering and terrorist financing.

There is, however, no uniform way to measure implementation. Unlike the UNCAC Convention, for example, the UNTOC Convention has no institutionalised review mechanism, and states have been reluctant to create one (Global Initiative, 2014). The UNTOC Secretariat, which rests with the UNODC, does not systematically record implementation of UNTOC provisions, e.g. on mutual legal assistance (Shaw, 2015).

Two useful, but limited, measures are the number of suspicious transaction reports (STRs) filed, and (perhaps more importantly) the number of investigations launched and resulting prosecutions (Table 2.9). Based on these criteria, GIABA members have some improvements to make.[2] This failure in practical application is replicated in a range of sectors, and reinforced by the findings of this report: while the requisite legislation is often in place, implementation falls short.

Table 2.9. **Number of suspicious transaction reports (STRs) filed and actions taken in response, 2013**

Country	Number of STRs filed	Actions taken	Result
Benin	8 953 STRs (all related to money laundering)	420 cases disseminated to law-enforcement agencies	No investigations, prosecutions or convictions recorded
Burkina Faso	65 STRs (all related to money laundering)	7 cases disseminated to law-enforcement agencies	Prosecutions followed in all 7 cases.
Cabo Verde	145 STRs (all related to money laundering)	32 cases forwarded to law-enforcement agencies	1 investigation, 1 conviction
Côte d'Ivoire	119 STRs (117 related to money laundering)	10 cases disseminated to law-enforcement agencies	Prosecutions followed in 11 cases.
Gambia	18 STRs (all related to money laundering)	7 cases forwarded to law-enforcement agencies	No investigations, prosecutions or convictions recorded
Ghana	398	32 cases forwarded to law-enforcement agencies	3 convictions
Guinea	None	None reported	Reporting entities do not yet generate STRs for investigation
Guinea- Bissau	145 STR (all related to money laundering)	38 cases disseminated to law-enforcement agencies	No investigations, prosecutions or convictions recorded
Liberia	47 STRs (22 related to money laundering)	1 case forwarded to law-enforcement agencies	No investigations, prosecutions or convictions recorded
Mali	22 STRs (18 related to money laundering)	1 case disseminated to law-enforcement agencies	No investigations, prosecutions or convictions recorded
Niger	19 STRs (14 related to money laundering)	6 reports disseminated to law-enforcement agencies	No investigations, prosecutions or convictions recorded
Nigeria	3 198 STRs (all related to money laundering)	61 reports disseminated to law-enforcement agencies	No investigations, prosecutions or convictions recorded
Senegal	128 STRs (127 related to money laundering)	16 reports disseminated to law-enforcement agencies	No investigations, prosecutions or convictions recorded

Sierra Leone	16 STRs (all related to money laundering)	No case disseminated to law-enforcement agencies	No investigations, prosecutions or convictions recorded
Togo	58 STRs (57 related to money laundering)	6 cases disseminated to law-enforcement agencies	2 prosecutions

Source: Abstracted from GIABA (2016).

Notes

1. Per the FATF (2013), the term *hawala* refers to a money transfer mechanism operating as a closed system within corridors linked by family, tribe or ethnicity. Used extensively along traditional trade routes in Asia, Middle East and East Africa centuries ago, in recent times the term has been used to describe a typology of money transmitters which arrange for transfer and receipt of funds or equivalent value and settle through trade, cash, and net settlement over a long period of time. *Hawala* and other similar service provider include hundi and underground banking.

2. Using the number of STRs filed as a measure of the success of Financial Intelligence Units is an easy, but imperfect, method. Having more STRs filed does not necessarily mean that a country is doing a better job at fighting money laundering: more STRs filed may mean that banks and reporting authorities are over-reporting for fear of being accused of negligence. Furthermore, more reports coming from banks in a region that is largely working in cash does not necessarily indicate that measures to money laundering are more effective: transactions that fall outside of the formal banking sector will not be captured.

References

AfDB (13 December 2012), "Urbanisation in Africa", AfDB blog, African Development Bank, www.afdb.org/en/blogs/afdb-championing-inclusive-growth-across-africa/post/urbanization-in-africa-10143.

AfDB (2010), *African Development Report, 2010*, African Development Bank, Oxford University Press, Oxford.

AfDB/OECD/UNDP (2016), *African Economic Outlook 2016: Sustainable Cities and Structural Transformation*, OECD Publishing, Paris, http://dx.doi.org/10.1787/aeo-2016-en.

Africa Progress Panel (2013), *Africa Progress Panel Report 2013: Equity in Extractives*, Africa Progress Panel, Geneva.

Audit Service Sierra Leone (2014), *Report on the Audit of the Management of the Ebola Funds*, Audit Service Sierra Leone, Freetown, http://reliefweb.int/sites/reliefweb.int/files/resources/assl-report-on-ebola-funds-management-may-oct-2014.pdf.

Blum, C. (2014), *Cross-Border Flows between Nigeria and Benin: What are the Challenges for (Human) Security?*, Peace and Security Studies, Friedrich-Ebert-Stiftung, Accra.

Briscoe, I. (2014), *Crime after Jihad: Armed Groups, the State and Illicit Business in Post-conflict Mali*, Clingendael Institute, The Hague.

Cockayne, J. (2011), *State Fragility, Organised Crime and Peacebuilding: Towards a More Strategic Approach*, NOREF Report, Oslo.

ComSTAT (2015), Common Market for Eastern and Southern Africa, http://comstat.comesa.int.

Duval Smith, A. (17 May 2014), "Mali flies into international storm over the purchase of a $40m presidential jet", *The Guardian*, www.theguardian.com/global-development/poverty- matters/2014/may/16/mali-president-boubacar-keita-private-plane-international-aid-donors.

European Commission (2015), *European Union, Trade in Goods with ACP West Africa*, European Commission (DG Trade), http://trade.ec.europa.eu/doclib/docs/2013/november/tradoc_151898.pdf.

European Commission (2014), *Economic Partnership Agreement between the West African States, the Economic Community of West African States (ECOWAS) and the West African Economic and Monetary Union and the European Union and its Member States*, European Commission, http://trade.ec.europa.eu/doclib/docs/2015/october/tradoc_153867.pdf.

ECA/HLP (2015), *Track it! Stop it! Get it! Illicit Financial Flows from Africa*, United Nations Economic Commission for Africa/High Level Panel on Illicit Financial Flows, African Union/ECA Conference of Ministers, Addis Ababa, www.uneca.org/sites/default/files/PublicationFiles/illicit_financial_flows_why_africa_needs.pdf.

ECA (2012), *Report on the Magnitude of and Tools for Measuring Informal Cross-Border Trade in Africa's Regional Economic Communities*, Eighth Session of the Committee on Trade, Regional Cooperation and Integration, United Nations Economic Commission for Africa, Addis Ababa.

ECA (2011), *Minerals and Africa's Development: The International Study Group on Africa's Mineral Regimes*, United Nations Economic Commission for Africa, Addis Ababa.

ECOWAS (2011), Directive C/DIR 1/o8/11 on Fighting Cyber Crime within ECOWAS, Abuja: Sixty-Sixth Ordinary Session of the Council of Ministers, Economic Community of West African States, Abuja.

Ellis, S. (2009), "West Africa's international drug trade", *African Affairs*, Vol. 108/431, Oxford Journals, London, pp. 171-196.

Faleye, O. (2014), "Impact of informal cross border trade on poverty alleviation in Nigeria: Kotangowa market (Lagos) in perspective", *Cross the Border: International*

Journal of Interdisciplinary Studies, Vol. 2/1, pp. 13-22, www.nepjol.info/nepal/index.php/CTBIJIS/issue/view/712.

FAOStat (2015), *Statistical Division for the United Nations Food and Agriculture Organization 2015* (database), http://faostat3.fao.org/home/E (accessed 25 September 2015).

FATF (2015), *Emerging Terrorist Financing Risks*, Financial Action Task Force, Paris, www.fatf-gafi.org/media/fatf/documents/reports/Emerging-Terrorist-Financing-Risks.pdf.

FATF (2013), *The Role of Hawala and Other Similar Services in Money Laundering and Terrorist Financing*, Financial Action Task Force, Paris, www.fatf-gafi.org/media/fatf/documents/reports/Role-of-hawala-and-similar-in-ml-tf.pdf.

Felbab-Brown, V. (2010), "The West African drug trade in context of the region's illicit economies and poor governance", paper presented to the Conference on Drug Trafficking in West Africa, Arlington, 4 October 2010, www.brookings.edu/research/speeches/2010/10/14-africa-drug-trade-felbabbrown.

Fortune, F., O. Ismail and M. Stephen (2015), *Rethinking Youth, Livelihoods and Fragility in West Africa: One Size Doesn't Fit All*, Fragility, Conflict and Violence Group, World Bank, Washington, DC.

Freedom House. (2012), "Country Studies: The Gambia", in *Countries at the Crossroads*, https://freedomhouse.org/report/countries-crossroads/2012/gambia#_edn3 (accessed 8 March 2015).

GIABA (2016), *Summary of Country Activity Reports*, 26th Plenary Meeting of the GIABA Technical Committee November 14-18, 2016, Inter-Governmental Action Group Against Money Laundering in West Africa, Dakar.

GIABA (2010), *Threat Assessment of Money Laundering and Terrorist Financing in West Africa*, Inter-Governmental Action Group Against Money Laundering in West Africa, Dakar.

Global Initiative (22 October 2014), "The future of UNTOC: Does unreviewed equate to irrelevant?", Global Initiative against Transnational Organized Crime blog, www.globalinitiative.net/the-future-of-untoc-does-un-reviewed-equate-to-irrelevant.

Golub, S. (2015), "Informal Cross Border Trade and Smuggling in Africa", in Morrissey, O., R.A. López and K. Sharma, (eds.), *Handbook on Trade and Development*, Edward Elgar Publishing, United Kingdom.

Goudsmid, T., A. Mancini and A. Vanegas Canosa (2012), "SSR, crime and regional development in West Africa", in Schnabel, A. and V. Farr (eds.), *Back to the Roots: Security Sector Reform and Development*, DCAF Yearly Books, Geneva.

Gubert, F. (2005), "Migrant remittances and their impact on the home country: The case of Africa", in *Migration, Remittances and Development*, OECD Publishing, Paris, http://dx.doi.org/10.1787/9789264013896-en.

Harding, A., G. Pálsson and G. Raballand (2007), "Port and maritime transport challenges in West and Central Africa", *SSATP Working Paper,* No. 84, May 2007, World Bank, Washington, DC.

International Centre for Trade and Sustainable Development (21 January 2015), "West Africa starts implementing the common external tariff", Bridges Africa blog, https://www.ictsd.org/bridges-news/bridges-africa/news/west-africa-starts-implementing-the-common-external-tariff.

IFAD (n.d.), "Remittances: Africa", webpage, International Fund for Agricultural Development, Rome, www.ifad.org/remittances/maps/africa.htm (accessed 25 June 2015).

IIAG (2014), *IIAG 2014: Accountability, West Africa*, Ibrahim Index of African Governance, Mo Ibrahim Foundation, www.moibrahimfoundation.org/iiag (accessed 8 March 2015).

Kaufmann, D., A. Kraay and M. Maastruzzi (2013), *Worldwide Governance Indicators* (database), http://info.worldbank.org/governance/wgi/index.aspx#reports (accessed 8 March 2015).

Krätli, S., J. Swift and A. Powell (2014), *Saharan Livelihoods: Development and Conflict*, Saharan Knowledge Exchange, December 2014, World Bank, Washington, DC.

Mailey, J.R. (2015), *The Anatomy of the Resource Curse: Predatory Investment in Africa's Extractive Industries*, May 2015, Africa Centre for Strategic Studies, Washington, DC.

Marc, A., N. Verjee and S. Mogaka, (2015), *The Challenge of Stability and Security in West Africa*, Africa Development Forum Series, World Bank, Washington, DC.

Mbaye, M. (2014), *The Informal Sector, Growth, Employment and Sustainable Development – Discussion Note, The Informal Sector, Employment and Structural Transformation – Some Operational Recommendations for a Productive Policy*, International Organisation of La Francophonie, Paris.

Meagher, K. (2005), "Social capital or analytical liability? Social networks and African informal economies", *Global Networks*, Vol. 5/3, Blackwell Publishing Ltd & Global Networks Partnership, pp. 217-238.

Mo Ibrahim Foundation (2016), *2016 Ibrahim Index of African Governance*, Mo Ibrahim Foundation, London, www.moibrahimfoundation.org/iiag/downloads.

OECD (2014), *Development Co-operation Report 2014: Mobilising Resources for Sustainable Development*, OECD Publishing, Paris. http://dx.doi.org/10.1787/dcr-2014-en.

OECD/EUIPO (2017), *Mapping the Real Routes of Trade in Fake Goods*, OECD Publishing, Paris. http://dx.doi.org/10.1787/9789264278349-en.

OECD/SWAC (2015) *Africopolis: A Comprehensive and Comparable Dataset on Urbanisation in West Africa*, Sahel and West Africa Club (database), OECD, Paris, www.oecd.org/swac/ourwork/africapolis.htm (accessed 22 September 2015).

OECD (2014), *An Atlas of the Sahara-Sahel: Geography, Economics and Security*, OECD Publishing, Paris, http://dx.doi.org/10.1787/9789264222359-en.

Population Pyramid of the World (2017), website, https://www.populationpyramid.net (accessed 20 September 2017).

Reitano, T., P. Knoope and I. Ustinoff (2016), *Final Review of the CT Sahel Project, 2011-16*, European Commission, Brussels.

Reitano, T. and M. Shaw (2015), *Fixing a Fractured State? Breaking the Cycles of Crime, Corruption and Conflict in Mali and the Sahel*, Global Initiative against Transnational Organized Crime, Geneva.

Reitano, T. and M. Shaw (2014), *People's Perceptions of Organised Crime in West Africa and the Sahel*, Institute for Security Studies, Pretoria.

Reporters Without Borders (2016), *Press Freedom Index*, Reporters Without Borders, Paris, https://rsf.org/en/ranking/2016.

Scheele, J. (2012), *Smugglers and Saints of the Sahara*, Cambridge, Cambridge University Press, Cambridge.

Shaw, M. (2015), "Global governance and organised crime: The United Nations Office on Drugs and Crime and the UN Convention against Transnational Organised Crime", *German Review on the United Nations*, Vol. 63/2.

Shaw, M. and T. Reitano (2014), *The Political Economy of Trafficking and Trade in the Sahara: Instability and Opportunities*, Saharan Knowledge Exchange, December 2014, World Bank, Washington, DC.

START (2017), *Global Terrorism Database* (database), START, Washington, DC, www.start.umd.edu/gtd (accessed 9 April 2017).

Transparency International (2016), *Corruption Perception Index 2016*, Transparency International, Berlin, www.transparency.org/cpi2016/results.

Uexkull, E. (2012), "Regional trade and employment in ECOWAS", in *Policy Priorities for International Trade and Jobs*, OECD Publishing, Paris.

United Nations (2015), *Transforming Our World: 2030 Agenda for Sustainable Development*, United Nations, New York.

UNCTAD (2013), *Economic Development in Africa, 2013: Inter-African Trade, Unlocking Private Sector Dynamism*, United Nations Conference on Trade and Development, Geneva.

UNDP (2014), *Human Development Index 2014*, United Nations Development Programme, New York, http://hdr.undp.org/en/content/table-1-human-development-index-and-its-components.

UN Comtrade (2017), *UN comtrade* (database), https://comtrade.un.org/db/default.aspx (accessed 20 September 2017).

UNODC (2013), *Transnational Organized Crime in West Africa: A Threat Assessment*, United Nations Office on Drugs and Crime, Vienna.

US Department of State (2016), *International Narcotics Control Strategy Report*, Vol. II, United States Department of State Bureau for International Narcotics and Law Enforcement Affairs, Washington, DC.

Van den Bersselaar, D., and S. Decker (2011), "No longer at ease: Corruption as an institution in West Africa", *International Journal of Public Administration*, Vol. 34/11, Taylor & Francis online, pp. 741-752.

WACD (2014), *Not Just in Transit: Drugs, the State and Society in West Africa*, West Africa Commission on Drugs, Geneva.

Watkins, K. and M. Quattri (2014), *Lost in Intermediation: How Excessive Charges Undermine the Benefits of Remittances for Africa*, Overseas Development Institute, London.

World Economic Forum (2014), *Global Competitiveness Report 2014-15*, World Economic Forum, Geneva, www3.weforum.org/docs/WEF_GlobalCompetitivenessReport_2014-15.pdf.

World Bank (2017a), *World Development Indicators 2017*, World Bank, Washington, DC.

World Bank (2017b), *World Governance Indicators 2017*, World Bank, Washington, DC, http://info.worldbank.org/governance/wgi/#home.

World Bank (2011), *Remittance Markets in Africa*, World Bank, Washington, DC.

Interviews

NE-Gov-LE-220915: Chief of Investigations, National Police, Niger, in person, 22 September 2015.

SEN-GIABA-130515: Multiple senior research and policy officers, GIABA, in person, 13 May 2015.

UK-Gov-LE-220615: UK law enforcement officials working on IFFs and Africa, in person, 22 June 2015.

WA-IOM-130515: Immigration and Border Management Specialist, IOM, interviewed in Dakar, 13 May 2015.

WA-CivSoc-130515, multiple, West Africa Office, Institute for Security Studies, interviewed in person, 13 May 2015.

Chapter 3.

Criminal economies and illicit financial flows in West Africa

This report has identified several often overlapping or mutually reinforcing criminal economies operating in West Africa. They use different methods, and are enabled by networks of both domestic and international actors. This chapter proposes an analytical framework for understanding the implications of criminal economies and their IFFs, based on three factors: where the good is sourced and whether there is a local market; the actors or networks involved; and where the IFFs are earned and invested. Applying this analytical framework conveys the nature and scope of the criminal economy in question, the underlying actors, interests and incentives behind it and the priority for harm-mitigating responses. It then provides a brief look at 13 different forms of criminal economies, according to a three-part typology: illegal activities, illicit trade in legal goods and illicit resource extraction. Each case provides an overview of the scale of the flow, the geographic area of vulnerability, the key actors involved, and the implications and impacts of illicit financial flows.

Introduction

A wide range of criminal economies are operating in West Africa. They involve different operating modes, networks and actors (both domestic and international), and are prevalent in different states and locations across the region. The illicit profits generated by these criminal economies also exit the formal economy through different means as illicit financial flows (IFFs).

Both directly and indirectly, criminal economies and their associated IFFs reduce the physical security, well-being and productive opportunities of West African citizens. Criminal economies are often underpinned and sustained by violence, exacerbating insecurity for ordinary citizens, particularly women and youth. Profits from illicit trade can further enrich groups involved in ongoing conflicts, including terrorism, and act as a potent driver of conflict, thereby undermining the potential for development. This environment simultaneously constrains legitimate economic growth, which acts as a disincentive for both domestic and foreign actors to invest, and allows criminality to thrive. At the same time, unchecked exploitation of the region's natural resources is causing irreparable damage to ecosystems, the environment and the livelihoods that depend on them, exacerbating the long-term fragility of the region as a whole. This study demonstrates the Gordian Knot of mutually reinforcing political, economic, social and developmental challenges facing the West African region. It also highlights the risks of simply falling back onto border-control strategies and law enforcement, which alone cannot effectively address the multi-dimensional nature of the threat.

This chapter establishes an analytical framework for understanding and prioritising the harms arising from criminal economies, thereby enabling a range of actors (national governments, regional actors and international partners) to better identify where they can apply their own set of responses. It then provides a brief overview of the major forms of criminal economies in the region, the scale of the flow, the geographic area of vulnerability, the key actors involved, and the implications and impacts of IFFs. To facilitate the analysis, the chapter breaks down criminal economies into three categories that align with the conceptual framework presented in Chapter 1: illegal activities, illicit trade in normally legal goods and illicit resource extraction. This typology divides criminal economies according to the nature of the good and practice, whether it is inherently illegal, and whether the traded commodity is generated inside or outside of the region. It also examines the extent to which it has a local market.

The next section draws on the findings of the report to propose a new framework featuring the five dimensions of harm. This framework may allow policy makers to rank the different forms of harm to inform policy design.

A development framework for analysing harm

Studies of criminology, sociology and development have put forth several ways of categorising and quantifying harm, with varying degrees of complexity (Dorn and Van der Bunt, 2012). The definition of harm also depends on perspective: different harms are experienced by different stakeholders – upstream, midstream and downstream – and in source, transit and destination countries. Thus, it is important for development actors to analyse harm through the lens of development objectives, as well as their own mandate to respond effectively to criminal economies and IFFs. A recent assessment (Global Initiative, 2014a) found that organised crime serves as a cross-cutting spoiler to achieving the Sustainable Development Goals by 2030, and a serious threat to attaining several core goals related to health, the environment, and peaceful and stable societies.

Development objectives can be grouped into five broad areas, which can be commonly identified and provide a useful lens for further analysis. These harms or impacts can be analysed and felt at the individual, community, national or international level, albeit with differences based on demographics, gender and individual or group vulnerability.

These harms are:

- **Physical:** harm to persons (homicides, violent crime) or physical infrastructure (damage to property).
- **Societal:** harm that creates or exacerbates societal tensions (including by inciting violent conflict, targeting individuals or groups on the basis of their ethnicity, identity or gender), and engenders economic or social marginalisation or exclusion.
- **Economic:** direct or indirect harms including IFFs that draw funds away from the legitimate economy, or divert resources to prevent or respond to criminally motivated harms, or to treat and compensate its victims. Indirect harms include damages to the economic climate, competitiveness, and investment and entrepreneurship cultures.
- **Environmental:** harm to the environment resulting from the unsustainable use of environmental resources, as well as damage to the environment caused by the by-products of criminal activity.
- **Structural/governance:** harm having a detrimental effect on the rule of law or the quality of governance owing to corruption, as well as the erosion of the state's reputation, legitimacy and authority.

The forthcoming case studies clearly demonstrate that different criminal economies in West Africa manifest themselves through different types of harm; all of the above categorisations can be found in one way or another in the region. Without a more granular analysis focusing on the specific criminal economy, the political-economy context and the respondent, it is not possible to argue that one type of harm is more important, dangerous or urgent than another. In fact, all stakeholders need to participate in this assessment, and the result will accordingly determine a shared course of action.

The nature of harm is subjective: moral and societal values both contribute to perceptions of what is "harmful". Although they are perhaps desirable, there are no existing universal standards to be applied. What some nations might consider as criminal activity may not be viewed as such locally. When analysing and programming development co-operation, caution should be taken not to demonise what may be less than ideal or create new problems for which no solution readily exists. Aggressive moves to change these business practices, or prevent them altogether, must be accompanied by moves to replace them with alternative sustainable livelihoods; failing that, vulnerability will increase. A more appropriate response might be to enhance social protections for the individuals most exposed – typically the frontline workers – through better monitoring and oversight, offering government subsidies to replace those offered by opportunistic criminal networks, and gradually shifting these essentially informal economies into the formal sector.

Towards a prioritisation framework

Again, an analysis of criminal economies and IFFs in West Africa identifies three major determinants of their impact: (i) whether the good is sourced locally or externally, and whether there is a local market; (ii) the actors and networks involved; and (iii) how IFFs are earned and where they are invested. These questions are best analysed congruently, to determine the extent and nature of the harm.

(i) Where is the good sourced, and is there a local market?

Establishing where the goods are sourced is an important factor for determining the likely harm or impact of a given activity. When a good is sourced and traded close to home, the extent of the harm on the domestic economy in question is likely to be greater, given the range of local actors and interests who are likely involved. It is equally important to know whether there is a local market demand for those goods, as it will signal the level of engagement of the local population and the economic importance of that illicit activity, i.e. the extent to which it may be a source of livelihoods within the local economy. Do the goods have value for local consumers? Will local communities be invested in protecting their continued flow as an invaluable and potentially irreplaceable source of local income and employment? Asking these questions can help host governments better assess the likely success of potential measures seeking to address them.

(ii) Who are the actors and networks involved in the illicit trade or economy?

This is an important political-economy question, designed to examine the underlying agency and incentives associated with the specific activity and ascertain which individuals may be involved (e.g. public, private, entrepreneurial or criminal interests; communal, traditional or even faith-based networks); how heavily invested they are in the illicit activity; the extent of their influence (i.e. their access and control over the criminal economy); and the nature of their public and private interactions (e.g. do they interact with political figures, senior public officials, private-sector or entrepreneurial persons, and regional or international interests). Understanding these dynamics will enable policy actors to respond by crafting better tailored policies that have some likelihood of success.

(iii) Where is the IFF earned and invested?

The impact of a criminal economy – and hence the response required – largely depends on how the IFFs generated by the activity are earned and where they are invested. This study found that regardless of how they are earned, IFFs that remain in the community, country or region contribute to the informal economy, even when they are clearly illegal (i.e. cybercrime); this has important development consequences. On the one hand, tackling or diminishing these activities could prove difficult, because they generate local public goods (e.g. local services and secondary employment). On the other hand, these activities could be seen as displacing existing local-market activities, or spiriting away resources that could have benefitted the local community. In short, the nature of the revenues earned, and their subsequent investment, will dictate the feasibility or likely success of interventions aiming to address them.

Regardless of how they are earned – and even if they are outright illegal – IFFs that remain in the community, country or region contribute to informal economic activity. Understood in this way, they can be seen as distorting local market forces, as they impact legitimate industries and the formal sector. At the same time, they generate income locally, which will grow the economy as a whole and create livelihood opportunities. If sustainable, these livelihood opportunities will attract people from across the region.

Where IFFs generate local income, they invariably garner the protection of those to whom the income accrues, who are likely to resist – including through violence or protest – efforts to restrict their income. Criminal economies with local markets and locally invested IFFs also typically play into local power hierarchies, resourcing and strengthening the individuals controlling the flow. This is significant, regardless of whether a terrorist group is extorting a protection tax, or local businesses or politicians are being enriched by the flow. Local distribution of IFFs also accrues local legitimacy, particularly if the local market is significantly larger than other industries. This is an issue in all cases, particularly when it relates to industries that increase the risks of conflict or terror.

By contrast, industries whose IFFs are mostly accrued or invested abroad have an entirely different dynamic. The extraction of goods indigenous to the region is a net loss to the state and its citizens. This is particularly true when the resource is finite, and its illegal extraction has a potentially irreversible impact on the environment or species sustainability. If the criminal economy lacks a local market and the IFF value chain is realised elsewhere, the trade is predominantly a transit trade (as is the case of cocaine trafficking). In such cases, interventions may simply serve to displace IFFs travelling through particular transit routes towards a more favourable environment; an effective response requires tackling both supply and demand issues. Where the IFF is mainly moving externally, responses should target those who benefit the most from the flow: the producers at the source (e.g. in the case of counterfeiting), those that pillage the market (e.g. illicit fishing), the vendors at the destination (e.g. drug trafficking) or the gatekeepers to the illicit resource (e.g. government officials negotiating extraction licences).

Criminal networks have demonstrated their ability to adapt to changing conditions and define new paths. National authorities should consider the local conditions that have made this a suitable transit route. Even if one criminal economy or commodity can be controlled, it will not take long for another criminal economy to emerge if the same conditions continue to exist.

Building on the findings of the first report delivered by the OECD on *Illicit Financial Flows from Developing Countries: Measuring OECD Responses* (OECD, 2014), this report focuses on illicit trade, and the illicit financial flows and developmental impacts arising from it. When analysed together, the three questions outlined above allow decision makers to better understand the potential harm generated by the illicit or criminal activity in question. They offer insights into the way in which development actors can frame, prioritise and sequence their prospective interventions.

To a large extent, gauging the developmental impacts or harm generated by these activities is a subjective exercise. Not all activities are strictly illegal, and not all illicit activities are stigmatised as criminal acts. Some may be seen as entrepreneurial measures, or as survival and subsistence strategies. Although the following section distinctly analyses the different forms of illicit trade, these often exhibit a high degree of overlap and convergence. In many cases, the same actors and networks enable multiple forms of illicit activities. As such, any attempt to map the continuously evolving context of illicit trade in the region involves identifying a confluence of different threads in a vast, transnational web of activity. It also requires knowing how the threads connect and influence each other.

Illegal activities

At a global level, the scale of criminal proceeds in the region has been estimated at 3.6% of global gross domestic product (GDP); the proceeds from transnational organised crime resulting from drug trafficking, counterfeiting, human trafficking, oil bunkering, environmental crimes, arms trafficking and others equal around 1.5% of GDP. About one-half of this amount relates to drug trafficking (United Nations Office on Drugs and Crime [UNODC], 2011a). The proportion may be higher in the informal economies of West Africa.

Deriving the value of flows at a continental or subregional level is challenging. It involves breaking down those flows, estimating where the profits are derived along the chain, understanding how they are entering the formal economy through money-laundering techniques, and estimating whether and how much of the flows leave the national jurisdiction.

Drug trafficking

Three major illicit drug flows transit through West Africa: cocaine, cannabis and methamphetamines. The cocaine trade is estimated to represent the highest value.

Nature and scale of the flow: since approximately 2007, West Africa has become known as a transit zone for cocaine from Latin America destined for European markets. Cocaine is widely considered the "king" of drug trafficking, generating the largest profits of any other illicit market in this region, as well as globally. Because of the flow's high value and the lack of an indigenous market, cocaine trafficking has had the greatest impact of all drug flows on the region's illicit economy and stability (Shaw, Reitano and Hunter, 2014).

An analysis of the global value chain of the cocaine trade has shown that only a small share of the profits from cocaine are realised in Africa. As shown in Table 3.1, the 2009 cocaine trade flow was worth USD 34.8 billion (US dollars) in North America and USD 27.5 billion in Europe; the value of the cocaine trade in Africa was a mere USD 1.6 billion, with only USD 600 million remaining on the continent, and 62% being laundered abroad (UNODC, 2011a). Although these figures cover the African continent as a whole rather than just West Africa, there has been little evidence of cocaine trafficking in other regions, besides a small amount in South Africa. Thus, it is broadly assumed that most of this flow is at least initially landing in West Africa. As a result most of the profits from the trade are likely being earned in this region. The forthcoming case study on illegal narcotics transiting through West Africa estimates that West African actors earn only USD 40 million per year from the drug trade (OECD, forthcoming a).

Table 3.1. **Estimates of all cocaine-related profits laundered in 2009**

Continent	Gross profits (USD billion)	Profits available for laundering (USD billion)	Overall share laundered
Europe	27.5	15.1	55%
North America	34.8	20.0	57%
South America	17.8	15.1	85%
Asia	1.5	0.8	55%
Oceania	1.3	0.8	58%
Africa	1.6	1.0	62%

Source: UNODC (2011a).

Demand for cocaine has been stable, if not slightly declining in Europe over the past few years, and global attention has increasingly targeted the West African drug trade, resulting in greater interdiction efforts. Coupled with increased instability in the Sahel and North Africa, the 2009 estimates are likely higher than what is currently trafficked through the region. A 2014 UNODC report observed that the extent of drug trafficking in West Africa was hard to assess, and seizure rates were low, which has been attributed to corruption and complicity.

Since 2011, West Africa has become a prominent region for methamphetamine manufacturing. In that year alone, five methamphetamine labs were discovered and dismantled in Nigeria. According to seizure reports, methamphetamine has been trafficked from West Africa, either directly or through South Africa, to markets in Asia and Europe (UNODC, 2014b). Between 2007 and 2012, the highest levels of seizures of methamphetamines were recorded in Niger, followed by Benin, Ghana and Côte d'Ivoire. This indicates that both land and sea routes are used to disperse the drugs following their production in Nigeria and Ghana. In 2010, the value of the methamphetamine drug trade in the region was estimated at USD 330 000 (Bavier, 2013). Given the increased activity around the drug, and higher prices and demand for it in Asia, this value has likely increased.

Negligible information is available about the cannabis trade in West Africa, where the cannabis is of a lower quality than that produced in North Africa and not suitable for export to either North America or Europe. Produced predominantly in Nigeria, Ghana, Senegal and Togo, it is assumed to be sold predominantly in local markets. West and Central Africa number an estimated 11-31 million cannabis users (UNODC, 2011b).

Although the local demand for illicit drugs remains relatively low, there is considerable concern that drug use in the region is growing (West Africa Commission on Drugs [WACD], 2014). Profits from drug trafficking in the region are derived from the safe movement of the illicit commodity across the territory, rather than from domestic sales. A 2012 report singled out Nigeria as having significant levels of demand for cannabis and methamphetamines, and to a lesser extent, cocaine (UNODC, 2012a).

The extent to which the region is used for transit can change significantly year on year, depending on comparative controls of alternative routes. For example, the increasing role of West Africa, as well as East and South Africa, as heroin-trafficking hubs has been attributed to increasing controls along the traditional Balkan route from Central Asia to Europe (European Monitoring Centre for Drugs and Addiction, 2015).

Within the West African transit region, the criminal economies of the drug trade have concentrated around weaker states, in areas where state control is known to be low and it is easier to protect the flow. The innovation and relentless criminal entrepreneurism of the cocaine trade is particularly well documented. West Africa has gained a reputation as a safe haven for cocaine traffickers, and nearly all West African states have been accused of ties to the cocaine trade (Ellis, 2009). Nigeria has the longest history of drug trafficking: its status as a transport point for heroin was reported as early as the 1950s (Ellis, 2009); this is reflected in the country's dominance of the region's drug trade.

Seizure data between 2007 and 2011 indicated that most of the cocaine flow is channelled through the coastal states of West Africa, with corridors focusing on two hubs. Ghana is the entrance point of the southern locus, through which cocaine is taken to Togo, Benin and Nigeria before being shipped to consumption markets (Oxford Analytica, 2013). The northern platform has Guinea-Bissau as its primary entrance corridor, although Sierra Leone has also been used (Figure 3.1). Once on the African continent, cocaine is distributed to Senegal, Guinea, Gambia and Mali for movement to Europe (Madeira et al., 2011).

Figure 3.1.**West Africa as a transit hub for cocaine flows from Latin America, 2014**

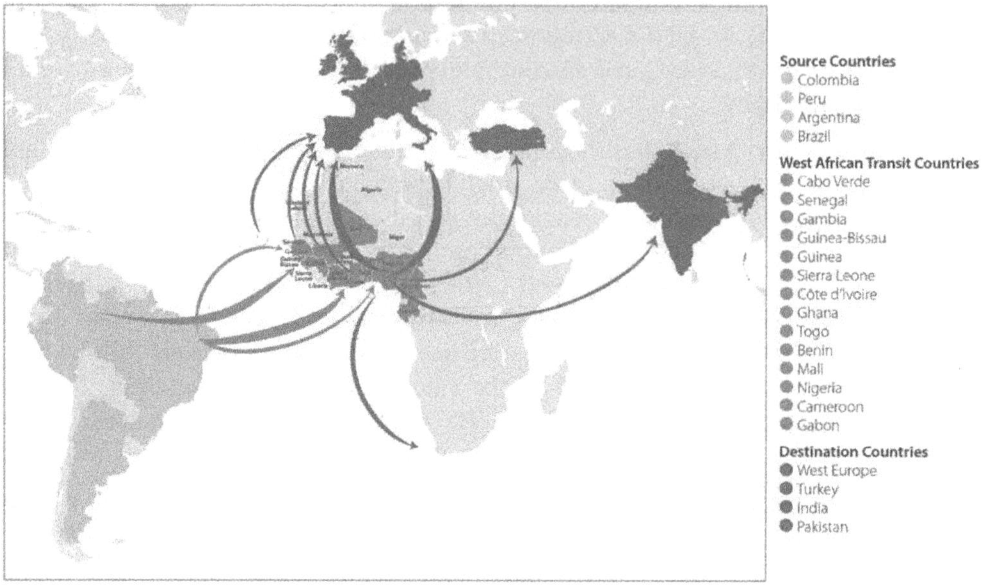

Source: Shaw, Reitano and Hunter (2014).

Over 2007-11, the largest volume of the cocaine trade through West Africa was conveyed by sea. A more recent UNODC report, based on 2012 drug seizures, asserted that cocaine trafficking is done mostly by air (UNODC, 2014c). A small proportion of the flow transits by land, moving northwards from the West African coastal states through Mali or Niger, across the Sahara to Libya and other North African states. Recent studies have suggested that French intervention in northern Mali only briefly interrupted (or diverted) this flow; it has subsequently resumed, shifting eastward as far as Lake Chad (Reitano and Shaw, 2015).

Key actors: Colombian drug cartels, as well as other South American groups, traditionally dominated the global cocaine market. When Latin American traffickers began moving their drugs through West Africa, the ownership of the drugs largely remained in foreign hands, and locals received only a small fraction for their logistical assistance (UNODC, 2011c). Under this system, the profits for West Africans employed by foreign criminal groups could be substantial: individuals could earn up to one-third ownership of cocaine shipments. This "commission in kind" was used to feed West African distribution networks in Europe, and to develop a domestic market (Alemika, 2013). A number of ethnographic studies have observed that Latin American drug dealers originally sought partners at the highest levels of the state to penetrate West African coastal states, especially those who could control transport hubs or deploy military assets among military and political networks to protect the trade. This is the case in Guinea-Bissau, where the trade has taken root most notoriously (Shaw, 2015), as well as in Sierra Leone and Liberia (Vorrath, 2014), and other neighbouring states.

There is evidence that South American organised-crime groups continue to play a major role in the region. Recent trends, however, indicate that Latin American cartels seem to be transferring more risk and responsibility to their African partners: African organised-crime groups are moving up the hierarchy, and becoming more proactive and powerful in the drug trade (Europol, 2011). In parallel, local groups (including key political and military actors in some countries, and more traditional organised criminal groups) are taking greater vertical ownership of the lucrative trade, controlling flows from top to bottom. Corruption across West Africa plays a visible role in cocaine trafficking in the region, with high ranking and well-connected individuals in many states implicated in the trade (WACD, 2014).

Growing evidence suggests that criminal organisations involved in smuggling methamphetamine exploit West Africa in ways similar to cocaine traffickers (UNODC, 2012a). Seizures of methamphetamine emanating from West Africa started to increase in 2008; the substance was being smuggled into East Asian countries, predominantly Japan and Korea. Ultimately, however, little is known about the growing methamphetamine trafficking in the region. Until alarm bells are more aggressively sounded, national law-enforcement agencies will continue to concentrate efforts on cocaine and cannabis (UNODC, 2013a, 2013b).

IFF implications and development impact: cocaine, a commodity with an approximate value of USD 2 billion may be pocket change relative to the global market; in the small economies of West Africa, however, the amount is substantial. In 2009, it would have exceeded total GDP in a number of states, with significant impacts on the political economies of the countries in question (Table 3.2).

Table 3.2. **Gross domestic product in 2009**

Country	National GDP in 2009
Liberia	1.155
Gambia	0.9
Guinea-Bissau	0.825

Source: World Bank (2014a).

No systematic estimates of the impact of drug trafficking on economic activities have been made, but the available evidence suggests that profits from the drug trade have remained concentrated in a few hands. WACD (2014) concluded that only a few individuals – who appear to be at the top of the pyramid of political actors – generally benefit from the trade. There is minimal trickle-down to the local economy, as – consistent with the UNODC (2011) report – little profit remains in the fragile countries through which narcotics transit (WACD, 2014). Bribes to low-level customs, borders, security and enforcement officials have largely remained in the country in which they are paid, and are most often used to better their living standards (Intergovernmental Action Group against Money Laundering in Africa [GIABA], 2010). According to estimates laid out in the relevant case study, 80% of the estimated USD 40 million earned every year remains in the region, and is spent on local operations and patronage systems. The remaining 20% enter the formal banking system and are laundered through the region's larger economies, i.e. Ghana, Senegal or Nigeria (GIABA, 2010).

The literature documents the impact of illicit trafficking on governance, rule of law, and peace and security in the region (Ellis, 2009; Alemika, 2013; Bøås, 2012; Briscoe, 2013; Aning and Pokoo, 2014; Gberie, 2015; Howell and Atta-Asamoah, 2015). The funds generated by cocaine trafficking transiting through West Africa have reportedly been used to intimidate or corrupt government officials. Given the weakness of the region's justice systems, payments have led to a widespread culture of impunity.

By many accounts, drug trafficking, state weakness, political corruption and powerful criminal organisations are part of a seemingly self-perpetuating cycle. Illicit profits can be used to influence political processes, and this enables actors involved with criminal groups to stay in power and build on their organised criminal activity. State powers that are vested in the hands of an organised criminal group through entrenched kleptocracy can enhance the criminal organisation's power by harnessing the infrastructure needed – i.e. its roads, seaports, airports, warehouses, security apparatus, justice sector and international political sovereignty – to further the group's illicit business aims. The result is a self-reinforcing cycle. While social and political instability may attract a thriving drug industry, a drug-trafficking presence in a country can further increase corruption and undermine political stability (Alemika, 2013; Shaw, Reitano and Hunter, 2014; Gberie, 2015).

Besides the political dimension, other impacts have not been well documented, leading to speculation and anecdotal evidence on cocaine trafficking's impact on a country's development (e.g. on health, education or community stability). Significant investment has addressed drug trafficking in the region, dating back as far as two decades. These efforts, however, stem predominantly from international counter-narcotics regimes and focus on interdiction. The strategies initiated at the continental, regional and national levels may have expressed more balanced priorities; however, they have been under-resourced compared to the scale of the problem, with funding mainly directed at security and justice initiatives (Aning and Pokoo, 2014). The failure to build alliances with civil society, as well as non-governmental and community-based organisations, and to educate the population have been major lacunas (Asare Kyei, 2013). Although much analysis has focused on the weaker states in the region, the upcoming case study (OECD, forthcoming a) suggests that the greater, overlooked damage may be to the region's more established democracies.

Kidnapping for ransom (KFR)

One of the emerging crimes generating illicit revenue is KFR. Although it has tight links to terrorism in the region, KFR is not restricted to terrorist groups, and has become a favoured and opportunistic means for criminal groups to raise funds.

Nature and scale of the flow: KFR has evolved from a largely politically motivated crime, often involving the kidnapping of Westerners in the Sahel, to a criminal act undertaken for profit. In 2004, the African continent accounted for just 2% of the world's KFR cases (JLT Group, 2012). Since then, KFR cases have risen exponentially: in 2015, 13% of worldwide kidnappings happened on the African continent, mostly targeting local nationals (Control Risks, 2016).

KFR first became an issue in West Africa in 2003, when the Algerian Salafist Group for Preaching and Combat abducted 32 European tourists. The Government of Mali successfully mediated and secured the release of the prisoners. Since then, KFR cases, and the ransoms demanded, have increased; nationals of countries known not to pay ransoms are usually avoided or swiftly executed; criminal groups are prepared to hold captives for years until a ransom is paid (Reitano and Shaw, 2015).

Although KFR has increased in the Sahel as the region became more unstable, terrorist groups, such as Ansaru and Boko Haram in Nigeria and Al-Qaeda in the Islamic Maghreb (AQIM), as well as splinter groups in the Sahel region, reportedly use ransoms to fund their activities (JLT Group, 2012).

Key actors: KFR has great appeal in West Africa. It is a low-investment, low-risk activity. Politically or ideologically motivated groups have the additional benefit of sending strong political messages to the international community. Since May 2012, the United Nations Security Council (UNSC) has expressed concern over the practice.

In the Sahel, KFR is usually attributed to terrorist groups. However, investigations have shown that terrorist groups generally buy or commission a kidnap from a criminal associate (Reitano and Shaw, 2015). When committing a KFR offence, the criminal group generally follows a process involving target selection, planning, deployment, attack, escape and exploitation. This means that the group must identify a victim; plan the abduction, captivity and negotiation; abduct and secure the hostage; successfully leverage the life of the victim for financial or political gain; and then escape (Stewart, 2010). As long as the perpetrators control the victim, they are able to deter law-enforcement or military actions against them.

In Nigeria, a wide range of actors with different motivations perpetrate KFR. In the north, the terrorist groups of Ansaru and Boko Haram have targeted victims ranging from mid-level government officials to wealthy individuals and tourists. In February 2013, for example, Boko Haram was paid an estimated USD 3 million to release a family visiting a nature park in neighbouring Cameroon. The terrorist group is also notorious for mass kidnappings, including the high-profile abduction of more than 200 girls (Chothia, 2014). Nigeria's House of Representatives issued a statement in 2015 that around 45 000 Nigerians had been kidnapped since 2012. Boko Haram has abducted at least 2 000 women since 2014 (Amnesty International, 2015).

In the Niger Delta, militants kidnapped oil company workers to demand greater control of the region's resources, or express grievances over control of oil revenues or lack of economic development (Refworld, 2014). In the urban hubs of Lagos, especially Abuja and Jos, express kidnapping targeting high net-worth individuals has become a relatively low-risk, high-return means for criminal groups to earn funds (*The Economist*, 2013). Although KFR is generally not an industry-specific risk, some groups and industries – i.e. oil and gas, mining, construction and aid workers – are more commonly targeted, because they tend to operate in high-risk territories or because of their national affiliation (JLT Group, 2012).

IFF implications and development impacts: in the Sahel, ransom payments appear to have close connections to local and central governments in the region. A number of privileged ransom negotiators and intermediaries have emerged, often with close connections to heads of state (Reitano and Shaw, 2015); it is assumed they are taking a cut and feeding a portion back to their patron (Lacher, 2012). Ransom negotiators are known to receive 10% of the total ransom amount – a perverse disincentive to reduce the total amount paid (National Public Radio, 2014).

A direct correlation between ransom payments and election funding has also been observed in both the Sahel (Lacher, 2012) and Nigeria. Criminal groups associated with specific KFRs have been seen using violence and intimidation on behalf of specific candidates during local elections (Stewart and Wroughton, 2014).

Although the kidnapping aspect of KFR is often highly publicised, the same cannot be said for the payment of ransoms. The consensus among the international community is that paying ransoms only fuels further terrorism and loss of life (UNSC, 2014c). No recent, publicly available data has looked at the way in which ransom payments made in the Sahel or Nigeria enter and flow through financial systems. Both AQIM (Financial Action Task Force [FATF], 2011a) and Boko Haram (Stewart and Wroughton, 2014), for example, have relied for some time on KFR as their dominant source of funding. The connection to terrorism has complicated the ability to monitor and track ransom payments, as legislation countering the financing of terrorism has rendered the payment of ransoms that might benefit terrorist groups illegal. Hence, affected corporations and victims' families are forced to negotiate and pay ransoms through private firms; in the case of domestic victims, they may not report the incident at all (FATF, 2011a).

KFR is growing rapidly as a strategy for criminal groups to secure funds and is empowering terrorist groups in the region. Extortion through kidnappings, particularly in the Sahel, has become a new security-policy challenge. The increased use of KFR by insurgent groups has led to governments and policy makers debating the most appropriate response strategies – i.e. whether or not to pay ransom, and whether to negotiate for release or attempt a rescue – particularly as kidnappers are targeting nationals from those countries that pay ransoms (Reitano and Shaw, 2015).

Kidnapping appears to reinforce the links between politics and crime, and is a growing source of local insecurity. The growing number of domestic targets in urban areas means it is increasingly becoming a financially motivated extortion racket. Because it often targets wealthy private individuals, kidnapping discourages entrepreneurship and foreign investment, damaging the region's potential for economic growth. It is particularly difficult to address in environments beset by poor rule of law, weak police and justice institutions, and minimal capacity for economic regulation.

Maritime piracy

Maritime piracy and armed robbery at sea are growing concerns in the Gulf of Guinea, with significant economic and security implications. Beginning in the mid-2000s, piracy in West Africa was initially confined to the Niger Delta and tied directly to conflicts over the oil industry. In recent years, maritime attacks have increased, both in frequency and geographic scope. In 2012, piracy incidents in the Gulf of Guinea surpassed those in the Gulf of Aden; they now constitute a major threat in the region. The International Maritime Bureau noted that 41 of the recorded incident took place in West Africa, including 18 attacks in Nigeria (14 of them against tankers and vessels associated with the oil industry). These attacks still primarily focus on the oil industry, as it is the most lucrative; however, there are now attacks on a far wider range of vessels (International Maritime Bureau, 2015).

To be classified as piracy, an act must have taken place on the high seas, i.e. in international waters beyond the territorial waters and exclusive economic zones (or EEZs) of sovereign states. Attacks within territorial waters constitute armed robbery against ships, or at sea (Kamal-Deen, 2015).

Nature and scale of the flow: more and better data exists on piracy and armed robbery at sea than on any other form of organised crime. Nevertheless, reporting rates are low, as shipping countries are reluctant to damage their reputations or risk higher insurance premiums; as a result, 70% of attacks may go unreported (Oceans Beyond Piracy, 2014). The Nigerian navy estimates that 10 to 15 attacks have occurred every month in recent years; at least 15 cases of piracy are reported in the Niger Delta alone each month. Independent maritime-security agencies within the region estimate that at least one act of piracy is reported within the Gulf of Guinea every day, and that this number could increase to two per day (European Union, 2014a).

Attacks in West Africa generally occur during ship-to-ship transfers, with a view to stealing oil cargo and other high-value assets. Rarely do West African pirates employ the kidnap for ransom (KFR) model used in the Gulf of Aden. Estimates of the annual cost of piracy in West Africa range from USD 565 million to USD 2 billion; the strategic development plans of many countries in the region rely on hydrocarbon resources, sourced from or transferring through the Gulf of Guinea (Osinowo, 2015). However, most of these piracy-related costs are indirect costs to the countries or companies involved in insuring, protecting or responding to the attacks, and the resulting net loss. Most attacks are simple robberies of cargo ships, valued at only USD 10 000-15 000 each. Consequently, the pirates themselves are estimated to have earned a mere USD 1.3 million annually in recent years (UNODC, 2013b).

In 2006, attacks were scarce and concentrated around Nigeria's two ports, Lagos and Port Harcourt (which services the Niger Delta). Nigeria has remained the epicentre of maritime piracy, accounting for 80% of all reported incidents. As shown in Figure 3.2, however, attacks have extended both laterally along the coastline and farther into the Gulf of Guinea (Osinowo, 2015).

Figure 3.2.**Criminal incidents along the Gulf of Guinea Coast, 2006-14**

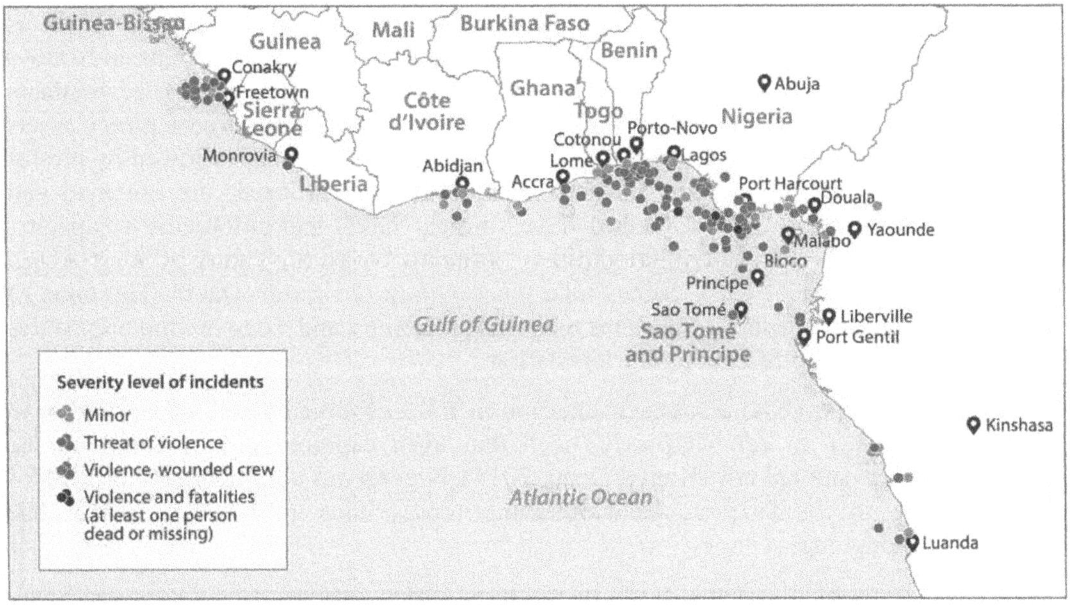

Source: International Maritime Bureau (2014).

Collectively, the coasts of Nigeria, Benin and Togo are at the highest risk of piracy in the region. Recently, attacks have put Côte d'Ivoire and Sierra Leone in the same category. Although the attacks off the coast of Sierra Leone are fewer than those off Côte d'Ivoire, they have involved high levels of violence (Kamal-Deen, 2015).

Arguably, the turning point for the expansion of piracy in the Gulf of Guinea was 2011. Previously, attacks on oil assets had been linked to overtly political motivations, i.e. the desire of Delta militants to see a broader distribution of Nigeria's oil resources. In 2011, the Nigerian government offered an amnesty to Delta militants, and the conflict largely ceased. The political rationale is still used to justify acts of criminality, both on land and at sea (see the section below on KFR), although the link is now more tenuous. Since 2011, attacks have become much more strategic and aggressive, even occurring in port areas (previously, a ship would be considered safe by the time it reached port) (Kamal-Deen, 2015).

What is more concerning is that efforts to strengthen naval capacity in the region have displaced it to an increasingly wider area. Operation Prosperity, the 2011 joint naval action between Nigeria and Benin, resulted in the first piracy attacks off the coast of Togo (Kamal-Deen, 2015). The largest span of piracy attacks along the Gulf of Guinea, with attacks as far south as Ghana and Angola, occurred in 2014 (International Maritime Bureau, 2015).

Key actors: the individuals committing acts of piracy in the Gulf of Guinea are local youth. The pirates are described as heavily armed and violent. They show signs of significant levels of organisation; hijacked ships often sail across maritime borders, where cargo is transferred to other vessels (International Maritime Bureau, 2015). Furthermore, given the nature of the cargo (see the section below on oil theft), local pirates require a connection to transnational organised-crime groups to ensure the onward sale of their stolen goods.

IFF implications and development impacts: piracy in the Gulf of Guinea is becoming more sophisticated. Associations with transnational crime groups indicate a widening spectrum of actors, including international investors, negotiators, accountants and foreign resources. Solutions that address the capacity to track and freeze piracy assets become particularly relevant. Cargo theft, rather than the KFR model followed by pirates in the Gulf of Aden, emphasises the need to identify how proceeds are obtained and laundered. States in the Gulf of Guinea have stronger naval and enforcement capacity, increasing the likelihood of interdicting piracy suspects. Given the nature of West Africa piracy, however, most of these crimes take place within territorial waters. The onus of prosecution, therefore, rests on the states themselves. Liberia and Togo are the only states in the region to have up-to-date piracy legislation.

A United Nations (UN) assessment mission in 2012 observed a lack of legislation in West African states to combat piracy, such that even captured pirates could not be prosecuted under national law (Kamal-Deen, 2015). Nigeria did not initiate the process of enacting a law to combat piracy and other maritime crimes until January 2013. The process is still ongoing.

In absolute terms, the actual costs of maritime piracy and armed robbery are lower than the huge losses incurred through total oil theft, estimated at USD 2-3 billion per year (see the section on oil theft below). Moreover, the regionalisation of the problem is having widespread effects on the economy and is increasing the costs of doing business in the region, both for importers and exporters. The wave of attacks in 2011 led international maritime-insurance adjustors to place Benin's waters in the same category as Nigeria's, increasing the costs of shipping to and from the country, and impacting on international trade and government tax revenues. The economic cost of maritime piracy in the Gulf of Guinea is estimated at USD 982 million in 2014; 47% of these costs are borne by the industry (Oceans Beyond Piracy, 2014). As the zone of vulnerability widens, so do the impacts on the region's states. The greatest cost is the weakened security of the Gulf of Guinea's maritime zone, enabling related criminal acts such as the trafficking of drugs and other contraband goods (United Nations Security Council [UNSC], 2012a), and the practice of illegal, unreported and unregulated (IUU) fishing (see the section on environmental crimes below).Yet the scale of maritime piracy is incomparable to the scale of illicit trade by sea through the region's largely unregulated ports. Limited resources, corruption within the port authorities, as well as the inability to physically inspect containers, provide a highly conducive environment for contraband shipments.

Cybercrime

West African countries play a prominent role in the growth and innovation of cybercrime. As a general rule, cybercrime evolved from the widely known advance-fee scams (or "419 scams") emanating mainly from Nigeria and Ghana to more complex operations perpetrated across a wider array of countries. The sprawl of first-generation cybercrime has already become so pronounced that the scam traditionally called the "Nigerian Letter" is now called the "West African Letter."

While cybercrime takes a wide array of forms, it can largely be broken down into three categories in West Africa: traditional criminal activity enabled by technological advances; first-generation cybercrime (the Nigerian Letter); and second-generation cybercrime.[1] These three types of crime illustrate that improved technology increases the efficiency of criminal cyber activity. Moreover, as more individuals gain access to the Internet, more people will have access to the tools necessary to commit cybercrime.

Nature and scale of the flow: cyber solicitations have been around for more than a decade. While public awareness is relatively high, significant amounts of funds continue to be lost to these schemes. Criminals have become adept at drafting requests and communicating convincingly with their intended victims. The growing prevalence of the Internet is also expanding the potential threat (Figure 3.3).[2]

In 2013, the estimated losses from 419 scams totalled USD 12.7 billion; over 78% of perpetrators were Nigerian or from the Nigerian diaspora (UltraScan, 2014). While Nigeria is the epicentre of cyber scams, the practice is spreading. Since 2011, 419 scams have been increasingly reported in other West African countries, including Senegal, Côte d'Ivoire, Cameroon, Sierra Leone, Gambia, Benin and Ghana (Boateng et al., 2011). More advanced iterations of cybercrime are also following in the wake of basic scams and frauds. The anti-cybercrime unit in Côte d'Ivoire reported scams totalling USD 6.2 million in 2012 and USD 6.6 million in 2013; a growing number of scams target nationals, as well as international victims (Kobo, 2014).

Figure 3.3.**Percentage of individuals using the Internet, 2002-16**

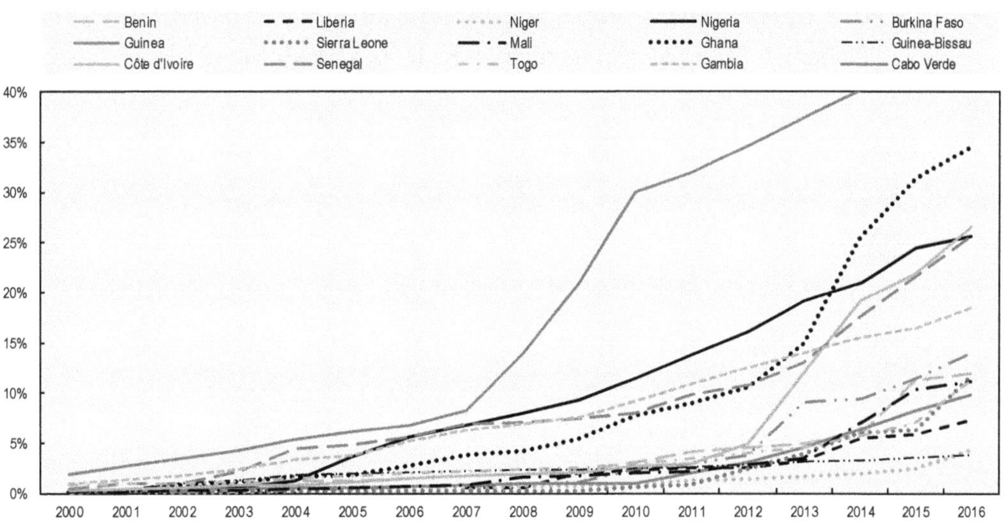

Source: International Telecommunication Union (2016).

Key actors: cybercriminals are mostly young males between 18 and 30 years of age. Although cyber criminality is becoming more geographically widespread and involves more nationals, Nigerians still play a major role.[3] Over 80% of cybercrime acts are estimated to originate in organised crime (UNODC, 2013c). The firms creating and perpetuating cybercrime are making it readily accessible and supporting its use, reducing the level of basic skills required for entry. Once perpetrated by individuals in cybercafés, cybercrime has metamorphosed into an operation organised by loosely affiliated networks working across several state boundaries and nationalities.

IFF implications and impacts: determining the true scale of cyber victimisation is difficult, as the crime is largely unreported, both internationally and in West and Central Africa.[4] Most victims so far have been international targets, thanks to their higher levels of disposable income and access to the Internet, but as citizens in West Africa shift away from predominantly cash-based economies, and begin to bank and transact online, the risks for people in the region will increase. Internet users in developing countries with low levels of cybersecurity awareness are also vulnerable to second-generation crimes, such as unauthorised access, phishing and identity theft (UNODC, 2013c). Cybercrime is a form of organised crime in its own right, but it also significantly enables illicit trade. The Internet has changed fundamentally changed the nature of criminal activity: it allows people to connect in new ways, facilitating all forms of crime, from drug markets to human trafficking and money laundering. It allows greater degrees of anonymity, making detection difficult or impossible. It also enables criminal groups to make transnational connections easily, giving them access to new victims, associates and markets.

The capacity to regulate and monitor cybercrime or cyber victimisation (or even Internet usage) across the region is extremely low, and limited information is available on the changing nature of the threat. Regional instruments include the Economic Community of West African States (ECOWAS) Directive on Fighting Cyber Crime within ECOWAS (ECOWAS, 2011) and the African Union Convention on Cyber Security and Personal Data Protection (African Union, 2014). Neither has jurisdiction in the region's countries, and neither offers resources to fight cybercrime (Table 3.3). In fact, the region has yet to legislate to render these incidents criminal acts.

Table 3.3. **Status of cybersecurity laws in ECOWAS countries**

	E-transactions	Privacy	Cybercrime
Laws	Burkina Faso Cabo Verde Gambia Ghana Senegal	Benin Burkina Faso Cabo Verde Côte d'Ivoire Gambia Ghana Senegal	Côte d'Ivoire Gambia Ghana Senegal
Bills	Liberia Mali Niger Nigeria	Liberia Mali Niger Nigeria	Burkina Faso Cabo Verde Liberia Niger Nigeria

Source: United Nations Conference on Trade and Development (2014).

Measuring the impact of cybercrimes resulting in IFFs across West and Central Africa presents further complications. Banks and other financial institutions are not reporting cybercrime, owing to fear of damaging their reputation and losing consumer confidence, and victims often do not report cybercrime because of embarrassment, or their own involvement in Internet fraud. They may also be popular figures wanting to avoid police and court attention (Boateng et al., 2011).

In 2009, MoneyGram International, Inc. paid USD 18 million to settle the Federal Trade Commission charges that the company had allowed its money transfer system to be used by fraudulent telemarketers to trick United States consumers into wiring more than USD 84 million within the United States and to Canada. Since then, money transfer operators have become more vigilant in protecting their services from online frauds (Federal Trade Commission, 2009). While increasing controls on financial transfers is one way to reduce the IFFs related to cybercrime, it comes at a price when it reduces people's capacity to access formal finance and banking services, pushing them into informal financial-intermediation markets.

Migrant smuggling

Following the collapse of the Libyan state in 2012, the nature of trans-Saharan migration to Europe fundamentally changed. The impact of these changes on the informal networks facilitating migration in sub-Saharan Africa has been considerable.

Migration in itself is not a crime, but many migrants employ the services of migrant smugglers, i.e. fixers who arrange passage either for one leg of the journey or the entire route. Under the United Nations Convention against Transnational Organized Crime (UNTOC), smuggling of migrants is illegal. Although often referenced interchangeably, smuggling of migrants and human trafficking are distinct crimes. Both human smuggling and trafficking involve the recruitment, movement and delivery of migrants from a host to a destination state, the difference lies in whether the migrants have a consensual relationship with smugglers, and whether they are free at the end of the journey (Shelley, 2014). The inclusion of these crimes as Protocols to the Convention indicate that they are both internationally recognised organised crimes.

Nature and scale of the flow: the number of West Africans migrating northward has steadily increased over the past three years, driven by conflicts in the Sahel, Central Africa and Nigeria, and by increased opportunities elsewhere. In 2014, Nigerians and Gambians were the most often detected nationalities, increasing more than 80% over the previous year and recording the highest levels ever registered for the region. Malians represented the third-largest migrant flow overall, after Syrians and Eritreans (Frontex, 2014a) (Figure 3.4). In parallel, over the same period, Italy reported a large number of sub-Saharan Africans of unidentified nationality (included in the "Other" category in Figure 3.4). Before 2014, hardly any migrants had been reported in this category; in the last quarter of 2014, 12 such detections were recorded.

A large proportion of the people of undetected nationality may come from the West African region. This spike in unspecified nationality could stem from the inability of authorities to register migrants properly, or from the fact that smugglers have encouraged migrants to avoid giving their real nationalities to improve their chances of not being returned. Importantly, much of the data and analysis on migration and smuggling of migrants predates the increased movement over the last three years, and assumptions underpinning policy making and responses may no longer hold true.

All West African countries are vulnerable to illegal migration, often motivated by economic reasons. Although West African migrants transiting Europe are the highest-profile migrant flow, migrants also target the Gulf States – albeit in lesser numbers.

Moreover, the bulk of Western and Central African migration takes place within the regions, and the numbers reaching European shores are quite limited (Kleist, 2011). In 2011, 70-90% of West African movement occurred within the subregion, where free movement in the ECOWAS zone makes it easy and legal. By contrast, 90% of North African migrants travel to countries outside of the region (International Organization for Migration, 2011).

Figure 3.4. **Arrivals by sea to European borders through the Central Mediterranean route**

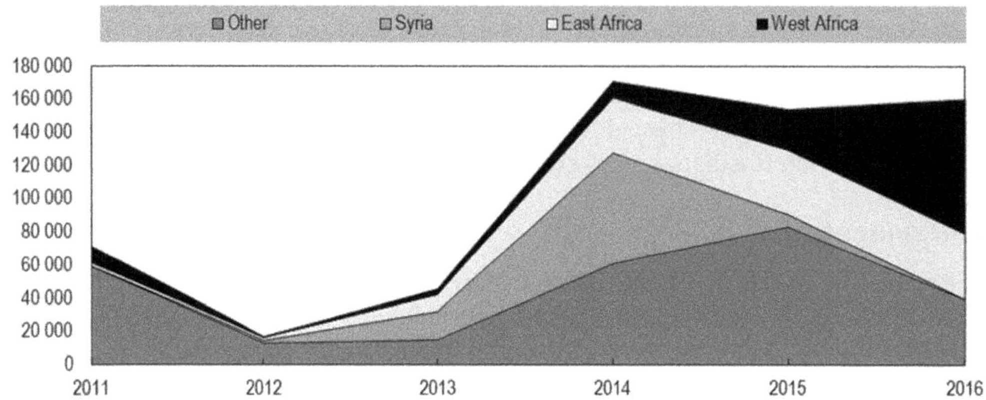

Source: For 2011-15 data: Frontex; for 2016 data: United Nations High Commissioner for Refugees (UNHCR).

Key actors: sub-Saharan migration has traditionally been characterised as "*ad hoc*". Smugglers are usually not part of well-organised transnational networks; instead, they act alone, or with a few partners (Shelley, 2014), or they work through clan and family networks.

The evidence also shows that a greater diversity of nationalities have become involved, indicating a growth in smuggling networks. Local smugglers appear to be more connected with international organised-crime groups. Reports suggest a growth in the number of smugglers from North African countries – Egypt, Morocco and Libya – as well as Turkey and other countries. These smugglers then recruit unemployed youth in Mauritania, Senegal, Gambia, Guinea, Côte d'Ivoire and Ghana to serve as recruiters in local communities (Frontex, 2014b).

When using the less sophisticated smuggling routes prior to the 2013-14 surge, migrants would typically pay each leg of their journey in cash, slowly progressing northward and often stopping to work to pay for the next leg (Shelley, 2014). Payments would be made to the facilitator of the leg, who would arrange passage and accommodation as needed; a fee would be paid to the transport provider; and typically a portion of the fee would be paid as a bribe to municipal authorities, the police or the town's dominant security force (UNODC, 2011d). Overland routes have become a significant source of income for many borderland regions, where local populations have begun to provide services to both the smugglers and the smuggled, including accommodation, food and frequently brothels (Reitano and Tinti, 2015). The abrupt loss of this collateral industry would impact on the sustainability of those towns.

More recently, due to the increasing flow and the relatively higher purchasing power of Syrian migrants, and the tightening of controls, smuggling services across sub-Saharan Africa and along the North African coast have increased their level of professionalism. Smugglers have developed specialised skills (such as document fraud) and commission higher fees from migrants seeking to reach Europe or the Persian Gulf. The heightened levels of conflict, and the proliferation of armed militia groups across the Sahara related to conflicts in Mali and Libya, further incite smuggling groups to carry more weapons to ensure safe passage (Reitano and Tinti, 2015).

IFF implications and development impacts: migrants are most vulnerable to exploitation, corruption or abuse when leaving the ECOWAS region to cross into North Africa. For Malian nationals, the move into the Maghreb is easier: individuals holding a Malian passport, or fake Malian identity papers, do not need a visa to enter Algeria (International Organization for Migration and UNHCR, 2011). The journey across the Sahara is full of danger: many face abuse, harsh conditions and even death. Often, the trip is much longer and more expensive than many migrants had anticipated, taking weeks or even years to complete, with many migrants getting stuck along the way. Survivors offer stories of setbacks, long waits without shelter, periods of hunger and thirst, and dangerous border crossings at night (Dixon, 2013).

It is difficult to determine the exact profits generated by the migrant-smuggling industry, or who is profiting. Earlier estimates of the total profit generated in West Africa amounted to USD 155 million in 2010 and about USD 105 million in 2011 (UNODC, 2013b). Given the increasing size of the flow in recent years, peaking in 2015 (Global Initiative, 2016), these figures are expected to have increased considerably. A 2015 report suggested that an African tribe heavily involved in the migrant trade in northern Niger and southern Libya may have been earning around USD 60 000 per week (Reitano and Tinti, 2015).

Understanding who is profiting is complex, and depends on the migrant's origin, desired destination and journey duration. Some reports state that migrants are forced to pay a percentage before the journey begins; their families are asked to release the balance when the journey is concluded. In some cases, the costs of the journey are repaid with labour at the destination – which for women, often means working in the sex industry. This exposes migrants and their families to extortion (UNODC, 2011d).

Until now, the economy around migrant smuggling has been largely cash-based, and the capacity to track resulting IFFs has been limited (FATF, 2011b). As more international networks are formed to measure and track IFFs, this should increase international capacities to identify and seize the assets related to migrant smuggling.

The use of migrant smuggling to facilitate irregular economic migration, and the services provided to facilitate it, have long been a local source of income. As the practice becomes more professionalised, and transnational organised-crime networks become more prominent, the risk of migrants being abused or trafficked will increase. Migrants often have their passports and all other items removed, making it incredibly difficult to obtain help or to return (International Organization for Migration, 2011).

While men are likely to be trafficked for labour, women are extremely vulnerable to sexual abuse and sex trafficking. Smugglers may force migrants to have sex with police or law-enforcement officials as a form of payment for letting them pass. Sexual assault along trafficking routes has been increasingly reported (Amnesty International, 2015). For example, non-governmental organisations, and the Director of the Ministry of Employment and Social Security of the Spanish government, have reported that almost all Nigerian women who reach Morocco have experienced sexual abuse before arriving at the reception centres. A number of cases of rituals aiming to tie victims to traffickers were also reported. A particularly violent group of "juju traffickers" was sentenced to jail in the United Kingdom for raping a Nigerian woman as part of a binding ceremony before forcing her to work in Italy as a prostitute (Frontex, 2014b).

Human trafficking

People do not have to cross borders to be trafficked. Human trafficking serves as an umbrella term for "the act of recruiting, harbouring, transporting, providing or obtaining a person for compelled labour or commercial sex acts through the use of force, fraud or coercion … People may be considered trafficking victims regardless of whether they were born into a state of servitude, were transported to the exploitative situation, previously consented to work for a trafficker, or participated in a crime as a direct result of being trafficked" (US Department of State, 2014).

For most jurisdictions in the West African region, the trafficking of adults is not a crime, although child trafficking – still widespread – is a criminal offence in all of the countries in the region (UNODC, 2014d). Many countries criminalise similar offences, such as illegal adoption, economic exploitation, forced services, kidnapping and rape, that often encompass human trafficking. This may mean that human-trafficking offences are being prosecuted, but as another crime.

Nature and scale of the flow: human trafficking is prevalent across West Africa; Côte d'Ivoire, Ghana, Mali, Nigeria and Togo have been identified as having particularly high rates of trafficking for the region (UNODC, 2012b). Especially vulnerable groups include persons with disabilities, albinos in rural communities and refugees (UNODC, 2014d).

Within the ECOWAS region, trafficking takes place mainly from rural to urban areas. Both men and women have been identified as victims of labour trafficking. The greatest number of internally trafficked persons were found working in the farming and fishing sectors, followed by working in servitude and subjected to sexual exploitation. An example of intraregional trafficking of women is the *Wahaya* practice, wherein a man brings young women to work (including to perform sex work) for him. This exists today as cross-border trafficking between Niger and Nigeria (Abdelkader and Zangaou, 2012). The trafficking flow also goes from the poorer countries in the region to the more economically stable countries: Benin, Burkina Faso, Guinea-Bissau, Guinea, Ghana, Mali, Nigeria and Togo are the main countries from which child workers are trafficked to the urban centres and agricultural sites of countries including Côte d'Ivoire, Gabon, Nigeria and Senegal, or to neighbouring countries in Central Africa (e.g. the Democratic Republic of the Congo).

Human trafficking is estimated to victimise 3.7 million people on the African continent, but the lack of comprehensive data and investigative research on the topic makes it difficult to measure the specific numbers in West Africa. The lack of border controls also makes it difficult to know when an individual is moving voluntarily or is being trafficked across borders. The available literature indicates that human trafficking is largely intraregional. Children make up the majority of victims, and labour is the dominant form of trafficking.

As with the literature on smuggled-migration flows, a disproportionate amount of reporting focuses on flows of sex-trade victims to Europe and more specifically, the conditions in destination countries. The data show that West and Central African victims were detected in 20 countries in Western and Central Europe, accounting for roughly 14% of the total victims identified in the region. Although Nigerians comprise the vast majority of victims, citizens of Cameroon, Ghana, Guinea and Sierra Leone were also detected. According to the United Nations Children's Fund and the International Labour Organization, around 200 000 to 300 000 children are trafficked each year in West Africa into forced labour and sexual exploitation (UNODC, 2012b).

Internal trafficking within the region is often overshadowed by the focus on transnational trafficking (UN.GIFT, 2008); as such, the widespread practice of trafficking for labour is broadly ignored in debates on human trafficking in West Africa, even though it often contributes to the supply chains of several international industries. For example, West African countries supply more than 70% of the world's cocoa market; Côte d'Ivoire alone represents 4%. This industry is said to be fuelled by the forced labour of an estimated 1.8 million children (Global Initiative, 2014b). Over the last ten years, INTERPOL has co-ordinated investigations into child trafficking in West African countries implicating the mining, agricultural and cocoa industries in Benin, Burkina Faso and Mali (INTERPOL, 2014a).

Key actors: the 2014 *Global Report on Trafficking in Persons* (UNODC, 2014d) establishes a typology spectrum for groups engaged in human trafficking, ranging from small-scale local operations, through medium-size subregional operations, to large transnational operations (Table 3.4). All are active in the West African region, although (as noted) with increasing professionalism.

Table 3.4. **Typology of the organisation of trafficking in persons**

Small local operators	Medium subregional operations	Large trans-regional operations
Domestic or short-distance trafficking flows	Trafficking flows within the subregion or neighbouring subregions	Long-distance trafficking flows involving different regions
One or few traffickers	Small groups of traffickers	Traffickers involved in organised crime
Small number of victims	More than one victim	Large number of victims
Intimate partner exploitation	Some investments and some profits depending on the number of victims	High investments and profits
Limited investment and profits	Border crossings with or without travel documents	Border crossings always require travel documents
No travel documents needed for border crossings	Some organisation needed depending on the border crossings and number of victims	Sophisticated organisation needed to move large number of victims along long distances
No or limited organisation required		Endurance of the operation

Source: UNODC (2014c).

IFF implications and development impacts: little systematic exploration has taken place into the linkages between human trafficking and IFFs (FATF, 2011b). Human trafficking is predominantly an interregional flow.

Human trafficking shares a number of linkages with other organised-crime activities. Smuggled migration and human trafficking often overlap. Human trafficking also has a close relationship with environmental crimes, especially mineral-resource crimes. Victims – especially children – are trafficked to mineral-rich areas and forced to mine. In October 2012, for example, an operation rescued nearly 400 child-trafficking victims, some as young as six years old, who were forced to work in illegally operated gold mines and cotton fields across Burkina Faso (INTERPOL, 2014a). As subsequent sections will discuss, the use of children in the fishing industry is also documented.

Children are also trafficked into military and rebel groups, where they are exploited as child soldiers. Child-soldier trafficking and small-arms trafficking are closely interlinked: both crimes have played major roles in regional conflicts over the years. Exceptionally, international companies may also be turning a blind eye to national labour regulation.

Illicit trade in "normally legal" goods

The informal economy generates considerable economic activity in the region, and is the income source for most non-food-producing households (OECD, 2013) (Figure 3.5). As described in the forthcoming working paper on the illicit trade in legal goods (OECD, forthcoming b), these goods are normally legal, but divert into the grey economies of the West African region. Consequently, a large share of the goods consumed, including significant volumes of contraband products (i.e. goods avoiding taxation and counterfeit goods), are sourced from the informal economy. The limited data provide no comprehensive estimates quantifying all sectors in all countries. Yet, should one aggregate the illicit trade in normally legal goods in terms of monetary turnover, it would by far comprise the largest single category of illicit trade in West Africa (as in large parts of the rest of the world).

While large volumes of illicit goods displace normally legal goods imported into West Africa, there is also production in the region itself. Asia is a major source of contraband consumer goods and medications, while North Africa is a source of smuggled subsidised goods. The Sahel smuggling routes have also helped West Africa function as a thoroughfare for certain imported goods, such as cigarettes (Shaw and Reitano, 2014), although low state capacity for regulation or control in post-revolutionary Libya has increased the likelihood of shipments entering directly through North African ports, making the Sahel land routes less attractive.

Figure 3.5.**Comparative values of trafficking flows, 2009**

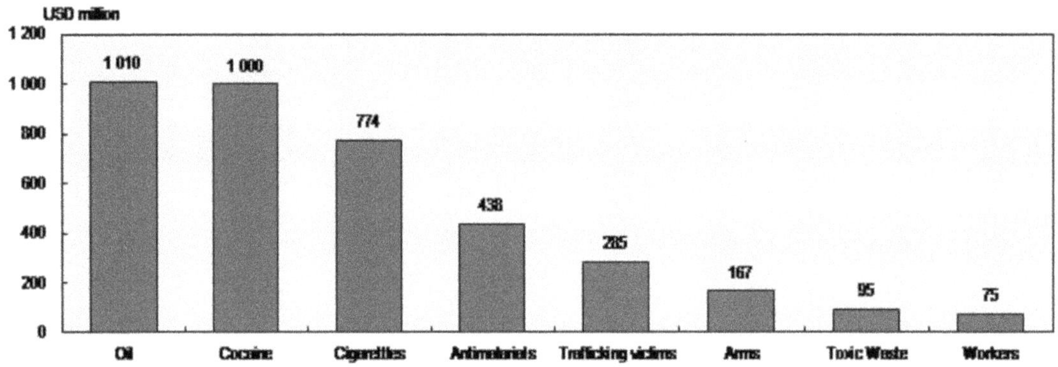

Source: UNODC (2009).

Medicines

As discussed in the forthcoming working paper (OECD, forthcoming b), substandard or counterfeit medicines are a significant problem in West Africa (Figure 3.6). According to the European Union (2014b), 60% of the market value of all medication in the region is estimated to be falsified or substandard. Estimates of the market share of counterfeit goods also vary widely. A 2009 study found that 27% of anti-malarial medication in Nigeria, and 82% in Ghana, failed chemical analyses; in 2011, the World Health Organization (WHO) found that 77% of Nigerian medications, and 64% of Ghanaian medications, failed to meet quality-control standards (UNODC, 2013b).

Nature and scale of the flow: the class of medication most affected in West Africa has been anti-malarial drugs. A 2012 study (Gaurvika et al., 2012) found that 35% of anti-malarial medicine tested in 21 studies across 21 sub-Saharan countries failed chemical analysis, and 20% of the overall total were classified as falsified. A WHO cross-national study found that non-compliant anti-malarial medicines were the most prevalent in West African countries compared to all other tested countries (Gaurvika et al., 2012).

In 2013, the annual value of counterfeit medicine imported into West Africa was USD 150 million (Mackey and Liang, 2013). UNODC estimates are considerably higher and suggest that the market for counterfeit anti-malarial drugs in the region was more than USD 400 million per year (UNODC, 2009). The Ghanaian sources interviewed for this study, however, claim that the Global Fund's subsidised anti-malarial medicines have reduced the incidence of falsified and substandard drugs.

Figure 3.6.**Share of anti-malarial medication found to be non-compliant with quality standards, 2012**

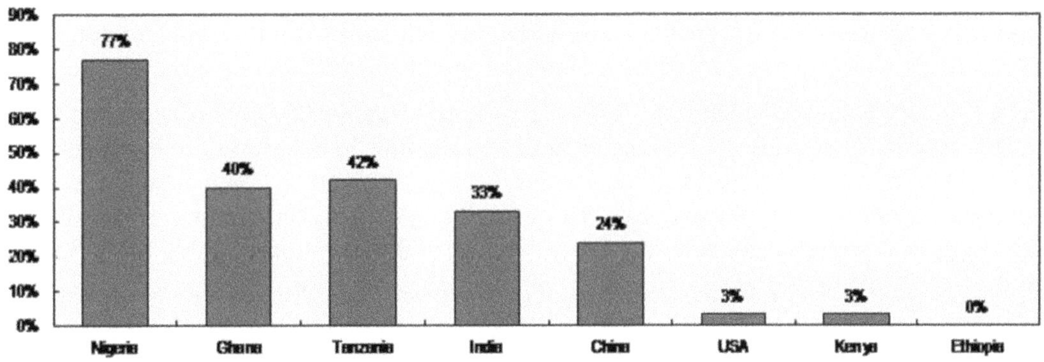

Source: WHO (2014).

West Africa is one of the regions most affected by malaria, and thus particularly vulnerable to counterfeit anti-malarial medication. Nigeria has by far the world's most severe malaria problem: in 2013, the country accounted for an estimated 37 million (18.7%) of the world's 198 million malaria cases. Other West African countries (Ghana, Niger, Burkina Faso, Côte d'Ivoire, Mali, Guinea, Benin and Senegal) were among the 16 countries that experienced the most deaths from malaria in 2013 (WHO, 2014).

Key actors: any discussion of counterfeit and substandard medication in West Africa should focus on two sets of key actors: those who produce the pills and those who distribute them. Companies in the People's Republic of China (hereafter China) and India are responsible for 70-80% of all active pharmaceutical ingredients, with China producing the majority (World Customs Organization [WCO], 2013). A 2008 investigation by INTERPOL and the WHO into the production of fake artesunates (the active ingredient in anti-malarial medication) seized in Southeast Asia determined that "all were produced in relatively temperate areas on the China/South East Asia borders" (Newton, 2008). The evidence from drug seizures within or transiting to Africa also supports the Asian connection: in 2012, for example, NAFDAC, the Nigerian pharmaceutical enforcement agency, seized 40 cartons of counterfeit Coartem (an anti-malarial) in a consumer-electronics store in Lagos. The tablets' shipping documentation pointed to a Nigerian trader based in the Chinese city of Guangzhou, home to street markets where merchants buy wholesale goods destined for African clients (Faucon et al., 2013).

As the region's largest economy, Nigeria plays a leading role as a regional distribution hub. In 2010, UNODC noted that "Nigeria appears to act as a clearing house for goods imported for regional distribution," including counterfeit medication (UNODC, 2014c). As noted above, Nigerian residents in China have been implicated in several large-scale counterfeit-medication busts. In 2013, authorities in Lagos broke up an operation involving the illicit import of medications, including Coartem, Ibuprofen and Maloxine, from China (INTERPOL, 2014b). In 2013, a customs operation co-ordinated by the WCO and involving 23 African countries seized 1 billion items, 49% of them fake pharmaceuticals (WCO, 2013).

Formal retailers (e.g. pharmacists) and informal sellers sell fake or substandard medications directly to consumers. Although not as important as producers or traders, they are much more numerous and play an important role in ensuring drug availability. Indirect actors also include intermediaries, who facilitate or enable illicit flows. For example, counterfeit or substandard shipments are transported by container. Payments for shipments – as well as illicit profits – are wired through banks or other transfer solutions. Consequently, illicit actors providing counterfeit or substandard goods largely depend on the ecosystem of the legitimate economy.

IFF implications and development impacts: dealing in counterfeit and substandard medications in West Africa is a lucrative business, without a commensurate risk of apprehension. In Nigeria, for example, as of September 2013, the maximum penalty for trafficking in counterfeit medication was a fine of 500 000 naira (roughly USD 3 000), and between three months and five years in prison (Akinyandenu, 2013).

First and foremost, counterfeit medications directly harm consumers. In 2009, at least 84 children were killed in Nigeria after taking a pain-relieving syrup contaminated with diethylene glycol, a solvent used in antifreeze and brake fluid (Polgreen, 2009). Counterfeit medicines also have a substantial negative impact on pharmaceutical companies' profits, costing the industry USD 75 billion in 2010 (WHO, 2010). The regulatory measures companies would need to take to reduce counterfeiting, and the security requirements to control networks engaged in smuggling, divert limited resources from other priorities.

The illicit trade in counterfeit and substandard medicine has other potentially severe global consequences. Counterfeit medicines frequently contain insufficient amounts of effective or active ingredients and are therefore often unable to kill pathogens, facilitating the development of disease-resistant pathogen strains. Near the border between Thailand and Myanmar , drug-resistant strains may account for as many as 80% of malaria cases – a situation attributed in part to the prevalence of counterfeits (McLaughlin, 2014). So far, Africa has been spared from infection by such strains, but that is likely to change if counterfeit anti-malarial medications remain prevalent.

The main linkage between counterfeit medications and IFFs is through trade fraud. Many of the schemes employed by medication smugglers to evade detection also defraud customs authorities. One technique used by smugglers is to list a landlocked country as the final destination for medications shipped by sea, allowing them to avoid customs inspection upon making landfall. After leaving the port, the shipments are simply diverted. Free-trade zones are also potential links in the smugglers' transportation chain (UNODC, 2014c); here, smugglers can modify the cargo, or alter documentation, without worrying about customs controls or import duties (WCO, 2013).

Although reliable data on illicit trade in normally legal goods are lacking, the scale of trade misinvoicing is thought to be significant. While this form of illicit trade is often considered relatively harmless, it has a number of negative impacts beyond the economic damage. Tax deprivation is the most commonly cited, but counterfeit medicines and substandard products (e.g. foodstuffs, and electrical and automotive components) also pose a risk to public health. These flows are often given lower priority by law enforcement, and yet they have synergistic effects with potentially more serious forms of crime, enabling smuggling routes to be used for other illicit goods (e.g. narcotics) or crimes, and they are also a proven a source of income for terrorist groups. The UNODC (2009) threat assessment for West Africa estimated that three of the four largest categories, in terms of value, are illicitly traded goods that displace normally legal goods.

Tobacco

In 2010, British American Tobacco (BAT), one of West Africa's largest cigarette suppliers, estimated that 330-660 billion illicit cigarettes were smoked worldwide every year, costing governments USD 20-40 billion in taxes and tobacco companies USD 5-10 billion in sales (BAT, 2010a). Cigarettes are lightweight and easily portable; many customs-interdiction programmes (e.g. drug-sniffing dogs) fail to detect their presence. Armed groups worldwide have funded their activities through the sale of illicit tobacco (Shelley and Melzer, 2008).

Nature and scale of the flow: in 2009, the UNODC estimated that illicit cigarettes generated USD 774 million in annual revenue in the region (UNODC, 2009). West Africans themselves smoke few cigarettes: despite accounting for 30% of Africa's total population, they smoked only 17% of Africa's cigarettes in 2009 (Maertens and de Andres, 2009). Even so, the levels of counterfeit penetration can be quite high.

Despite this high prevalence of illicit cigarettes on local markets, the region has been more important as a conduit for illicit cigarettes to North Africa.[5] Nevertheless, the ports of Lomé in Benin and Cotonou in Togo are among the two most important conduits for tobacco imported illegally into West Africa and generally headed to Nigeria, which has established high tariffs on tobacco. In 2008, Benin and Togo imported a total of CFA 31.1 billion (West African CFA francs) (USD 30-50 million) worth of cigarettes destined for re-export, much of which ended up crossing illegally into Nigeria (Golub, 2012). Smugglers in other West African countries also benefit from imports through Togo and Benin: in March 2009, a shipment of 32 400 000 illicit cigarettes was seized in Côte d'Ivoire, after landing in Togo and transiting through Ghana (WCO, 2010).

The other zone of major vulnerability is the Sahel, owing to the smuggling routes connecting West Africa to North Africa. The proceeds from the sale of these cigarettes fund the operations of several militant and terrorist groups (see below), enabling them to continue to engage in drug trafficking, human trafficking and other violent enterprises (Wilson, 2009).

Key actors: several globally renowned individuals and organisations are closely involved in smuggling tobacco through West Africa. Warlords in the Sahara have engaged in cigarette smuggling across the Sahel to finance activities under the banner of the Signed-in-Blood Battalion (Lacher, 2013) and have also been associated with several lucrative hostage-taking operations in Algeria, including the capture of employees at a natural-gas plant in January 2013 (Jenkins, 2013; BBC, 2015).

In Nigeria, rather than terrorist or other ideological forces, smaller-scale enterprises and individuals looking to make money appear to dominate the tobacco-smuggling industry. According to an investigative report by a Nigerian newspaper (Ogala, 2014) most illegal cigarettes imported into the country are transported by vehicle smugglers known as "Yan-Pitos", which pick up shipments at southern Benin ports and then drive north before crossing into Nigeria, either directly or via Niger. Nigeria's porous borders make this a comparatively low-risk operation for the Yan-Pitos, which also reportedly hedge their bets by bribing border guards and customs officials (Ogala, 2014).

IFF implications and development impacts: as cigarette smuggling is by definition illegal, it does not generally serve as an instrument for money laundering. It does, however, provide smugglers with significant financial resources. Most of the proceeds are moved to offshore accounts, whereupon the money is used for other purposes (FATF, 2012). The WCO notes that "[the] illicit trade in tobacco is an important predicate offence of money laundering." However, due to limitations on jurisdiction or capability, many customs authorities do not investigate money laundering related to illicit tobacco trade and focus instead on the smuggling itself (WCO, 2013).

The impact of illicit tobacco on West Africa is twofold. First, the profits earned by armed groups from tobacco smuggling have significantly helped them to continue their illicit activities. This has, of course, negatively impacted on the lives of law-abiding local residents, either directly (e.g. through kidnappings) or indirectly (e.g. by discouraging legitimate businesses).

More directly, the prevalence of illicit tobacco products entails significant losses in tax revenue. In 2014, the Imperial Tobacco company estimated that smuggling cost the Government of Mali CFA 10 billion (USD 16.6 million) every year (Imperial Tobacco, 2014). While specific numbers are not available for Nigeria, the large number of illicit cigarettes consumed in the country also represents a sizeable loss in tax revenue, given that cigarettes are subject to a significant excise tax.

Firearms

Illicit firearms and ammunition are normally legal goods diverted from the legitimate supply chain. In a region vulnerable to terrorists and serious organised crime, the availability of illicit firearms constitutes a serious challenge. If income from criminal activities is a prerequisite for the economic power base of criminal actors, illicit firearms and ammunition are a prerequisite for their military power. In the most extreme cases, these firearms can challenge the state's legitimate monopoly on force.

The West African region is awash in illicit weapons from countless sources, driving armed conflict and facilitating the commission of many other types of crime. In some cases, these weapons enter the region in small quantities through poorly policed borders. In other cases, large shipments are orchestrated by regional governments or other powerful actors. Even those illicit firearms that have been found and seized are not safe: the region's stockpiles of confiscated weapons have repeatedly been burgled. Thieves use these weapons to commit other crimes, or fight armed struggles; they can also turn in weapons to regional disarmament programmes or sell the surplus (Small Arms Survey, 2013).

Nature and scale of the flow: no reliable statistics exist on arms trafficking in West Africa. The Small Arms Survey's methodology underscores "the importance of developing – and using – an information gathering system to complement national reporting" (Carlson, 2013). A general picture can be pieced together from isolated data, such as those from Côte d'Ivoire and Liberia, both of which were subjected to arms embargoes during the 2000s. Embargoes help increase attention to arms trafficking in a particular country. By making all arms transactions illegal, they make it easier to discern which arms were trafficked, and which were legitimately acquired. Between 2005 and 2010, just over

USD 25 million worth of firearms were smuggled into Côte d'Ivoire; Liberia imported some USD 8 million while under an embargo between 2000 and 2010 (Oxfam, 2012). The other major external source of arms in West Africa is Libya: since the fall of the Gaddafi regime, as many as 12 000 weapons may have been illegally trafficked from Libya into Mali in 2013 (UNODC, 2013b; Shaw and Mangan, 2014).

More important than these inflows is the large quantity of firearms already available in the region. In 2004, an estimated 8-10 million illicit firearms were circulating in West Africa (Bah, 2004). In the decade since, those weapons changed hands. In the case of Côte d'Ivoire, for example, researchers have repeatedly found small quantities of unusual ammunition in circulation, suggesting that fighters simply reuse rather than import modern weaponry (Anders, 2014).

Few, if any, areas in West Africa are considered safe from the threat of arms trafficking (Figure 3.7): the multiple conflict systems across the region have provided millions of people with the means, motive and opportunity to acquire weapons on the black market.

Figure 3.7.**Major arms flows in the region**

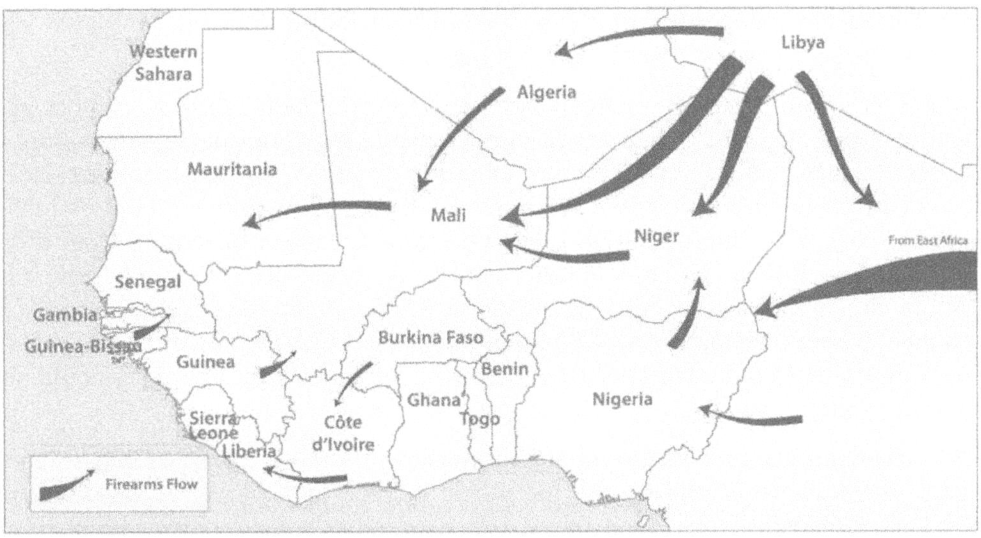

Source: UNODC (2013b), with modifications by the authors.

Nevertheless, some areas of the region are more vulnerable than others. Nigeria's long history of armed conflict, combined with the country's notoriously porous borders, has made it a regional hub for arms trafficking (Onuoha, 2013). Two other prime locations for arms smugglers are the desert of northern Mali (Reitano and Shaw, 2015) and West Africa's Atlantic coast (O'Regan and Thompson, 2013).

Key actors: a wide variety of actors across West Africa are active in the trade. The first category are groups actively fighting an armed conflict. The Nigerian Islamist group Boko Haram, for example, has been caught smuggling guns into Nigeria (IRIN News, 2014a). In addition, Malian rebels have imported weaponry from Libya and other sources (Small Arms Survey, 2013).

A second category of key actors is small-time smugglers and weapons dealers. All across the region, people unaffiliated with groups fighting in armed conflicts regularly smuggle weapons for a variety of reasons. In Liberia, the United Nations has reported that agricultural communities traffic 12-gauge shotguns from Guinea for hunting, although they are also used in robberies (UNSC, 2013a). As the level of violence has increased in the Sahel and Maghreb, those involved in illicit trade possess more arms to protect their goods; many traffic weapons as part of cargo transiting the Sahel to and from Mali and Niger (Reitano and Shaw, 2015). Several countries (e.g. Benin and Ghana) have robust local cottage industries producing artisanal firearms, many of which are trafficked as a way of earning a living (Ohene-Asare et al., 2014).

The third category of key actor is governments. Looking at ammunition with a shorter life span than firearms, manufacturers outside West Africa clearly play a role in maintaining the operability of military firearms held by non-state actors. For example, UN investigators in Côte d'Ivoire identified ammunition that entered the country in violation of the 2004-16 arms embargo as having been originally sold to the government of Burkina Faso (UNSC, 2012b). Just weeks before the imposition of the UN arms embargo, Côte d'Ivoire began acquiring firearms in violation of the ECOWAS Moratorium established in 1998 and renewed in 2001 and 2004 (de Tessieres, 2012). The evidence has also shown that the Guinea-Bissau government has trafficked firearms for its own use, as well as to supply the conflict in Casamance (O'Regan and Thompson, 2013).

Although governments – or at least individuals within them – play an important role in the arms trade, there are also cases of direct external deliveries to criminal actors. Ten pan-African investigations found Iranian ammunition and weapons in the service of a variety of non-state entities (Ohene-Asare et al., 2014); other source countries included Romania, Sudan and China. The 2012 UN Group of Experts Concerning Côte d'Ivoire established that Romanian ammunition had likely been diverted from government stockpiles in Burkina Faso, and that Chinese ammunition was likely diverted from government stocks in Niger. Chinese ammunition packaged in polyethylene bags also suggests diversion from Sudan after legal delivery, yet the means of delivery could not be confirmed (Anders, 2014).

IFF implications and development impacts: with the exception of certain conflict hotspots, the monetary turnover of the illicit market in firearms is unlikely to be significant compared to other illicit flows. However, it has a disproportionate importance in empowering criminal groups, insurgents and terrorists, who contribute to regional instability and the rising levels of violence.

Arms trafficking and IFFs are intimately connected in West Africa, as they are in the rest of the world. These linkages generally take one of two forms. First, arms trafficking may be used to generate revenue for armed groups. Detained arms traffickers in Nigeria, for example, have told police that the proceeds from their sales were destined for Boko Haram (FATF, 2013). Second, the revenue obtained from selling arms illegally may simply be kept for the benefit of the sellers: arms dealers in Nigeria have been caught trying to hide their gains overseas, or in Nigerian soldiers' bank accounts; in Senegal, criminals of various types have reportedly used the houses of arms dealers to store their cash (GIABA, 2013).

The illicit movement of arms perpetuates armed conflict, and undermines peacebuilding and development. By definition, armed conflict cannot occur without arms; the large quantities of readily available illegal weapons facilitate the escalation of local disputes into internal or regional warfare. In addition to providing ingredients for armed conflict, arms trafficking also plays a role in commissioning other types of criminal activity (Shaw, Reitano and Hunter, 2014). In the Niger Delta, trafficked firearms are regularly used in oil theft and piracy (GIABA, 2010). Côte d'Ivoire and Sierra Leone suffered high rates of armed robberies and vehicle hijackings in the 2000s, many of them committed with illicit firearms (Alemika, 2013). Arms trafficking has also played a key role in the rise of large-scale drug trafficking throughout West Africa and has allowed the development of powerful protection economies to protect those flows (Reitano and Shaw, 2015). All of this, of course, takes a toll on legitimate business and violence levels in the community, and thus on local residents' security and quality of life.

Counterfeit and stolen goods

While medicines and tobacco have received some attention, other neglected areas of criminal activity also include trade in stolen goods (e.g. motor vehicles) and other counterfeit or substandard goods. The wide range of criminal activities of this nature has implications beyond the region, with links being made between the illicit trade in vehicles, international organised-crime groups and terrorist financing.

Nature and scale of the flow: although it is not possible to fully identify the scale of the flow of counterfeits, anecdotal evidence suggests it is rising. These practices are not unique to West Africa; the discovery of a large trafficking ring revealed that the most popular destinations for vehicles are Ghana, Gambia and Nigeria (Golub, 2012). The ring also shows increased professionalism (INTERPOL, 2014c). In 2013, Togo, Côte d'Ivoire, Benin and Nigeria accounted for more than 56 million counterfeited items seized in one year, ranking in the top-15 countries worldwide in terms of intellectual property-rights infringement. The goods seized in the region ranged from household goods and electrical appliances to brand-name luxury goods (WCO, 2013).

Coastal states such as Gambia, Benin and Togo facilitate smuggling to landlocked countries (Golub, 2012). While goods are spread across the region, Nigeria, with its large economy, is a hub. For example, the rate of Benin's imports of second-hand cars rose from 200 000 vehicles per year in 2010 to 314 000 in 2014. Around 80-90% of these vehicles go to Nigeria; it is likely that a number of transactions are illegal, and that Benin and Togo compete to smuggle vehicles into Nigeria (INTERPOL, 2014c).

Asia and Europe are also implicated. Cars are stolen from markets in Europe, most notably those with easy port access, although some vehicles are stolen from landlocked states. In an impressive display of logistical capacity, a car stolen in Europe can take less than 24 hours to arrive in West Africa for resale (INTERPOL, 2014c).

Key actors: while financial gain is the common denominator of organised-crime networks, terrorist groups have also been involved. Cases involving vehicle theft and sales substantiate these claims, with arrests of Nigerian actors in recent years (US Immigration and Customs Enforcement, 2014). Given the broad nature of the supply chain, criminal groups in the region have connections to international networks to facilitate the purchase, transfer and sale of counterfeit and stolen goods. The nations with the highest rate of counterfeiting are China; Hong Kong, China; and India; China alone supplies over one-half of the world's counterfeit goods (WCO, 2013). Because law enforcement in the region generally grants low priority to these crimes, they have become relatively lucrative and low risk, providing an easy way for groups to launder money from other activities (SEN-GIABA-130515; UK-Gov-LE-220615).

Impact: the prevalence of counterfeit and other goods displacing normally legal goods in West Africa has multiple impacts. The three most important are lost tax revenues, lost sales for legitimate enterprises (domestic businesses, such as the textiles sector, or foreign exporters), and public health risks. Smuggling also contributes to a culture of corruption and tax avoidance (Golub, 2012).

Illicit resource extraction

West Africa is rich in national resources, and yet illicit resource extraction remains a particularly worrisome category of IFFs. These assets are indigenous to the region; while they play a pivotal role in the formal economy, they can readily be diverted into the illicit economy at various points of the supply chain (source, transit, sale and export), thereby generating IFFs. Rather than driving development, the story of the region's natural-resource exploitation is one of oil and minerals driving institutional corrosion, instability, violence and conflict.

Nevertheless, demonising the sector as a whole would be a misstep, with potentially detrimental effects on the livelihoods of a large share of the population. Most natural-resource industries in West Africa feature a degree of subsistence-level criminal activity, e.g. poaching for individual use, artisanal mining and small-scale tapping of oil pipelines. These typically comprise income strategies for ordinary people lacking credible alternative livelihoods; both the products and profits may be invested in the local economy. In fact, as artisanal trades are increasingly identified as an important driver of development, there is growing momentum to formalise these sectors.[6]

Oil theft

Nigeria is the world's thirteenth-largest oil producer; in fact, oil is the main driver of its prosperity (World Bank, 2014b). At its peak in 2012, the country was exporting over 2 million barrels per day (b/d) with an average daily value of USD 178 million.[7] Petroleum accounted for more than one-half of Nigeria's GDP, about 85% of government revenues and over 90% of exports (Gboyega et al., 2011). Yet the country's inability to control the integrity of its oil trade has made it the African country with the highest cumulative IFFs: Nigeria represents 79% of total West African IFFs and 30.5% of Africa's (HLP, 2015); this has spillover implications for neighbouring countries.

Nature and scale of the flow: estimates of the total scale of oil lost to illicit activity differ vastly – from 100 000 barrels per day (b/d) to 250 000 barrels per day – valued at approximately USD 3-8 billion per year (Katsouris and Sayne, 2013). The International Energy Agency (IEA) estimated that oil theft in Nigeria amounted to 150 000 b/d; this would comprise a loss of over USD 5 billion per year – a sum that would fund access to electricity for all Nigerians by 2030 (IEA, 2014).

Chatham House published the most in-depth examination of the illicit oil trade in Nigeria in 2013 (Katsouris and Sayne, 2013), describing in detail the methods used to divert oil. Some illicit trade consists in small-scale pilfering for domestic use, but most is industrial-scale bunkering to take the oil out into international waters and sell it in another jurisdiction (Katsouris and Sayne, 2013). The large oil tankers (licit and illicit) on their way to export platforms are also highly vulnerable to piracy in the Gulf of Guinea, which has become a rising threat driven by Nigerian oil (see the section above on maritime piracy).

Key actors: domestic engagement in Nigerian oil theft is extensive, and is based on has established organised criminal industries and protection networks. The Chatham House (Katsouris and Sayne, 2013) report describes networks as more cellular than hierarchical in nature, a logical route given the degree of flexibility this affords to those involved. However, a number of key personnel and operating factors remain (Table 3.5).

Table 3.5. **Anatomy of a typical large-scale oil-theft operation**

Role	Actions	Alleged common identites
High-level opportunists	Collect profits from theft by virtue of their status and ability to restrict and control others' access to the trade	Mostly government officials and security-force personnel; some traditional rulers and local godfathers
Facilitators	Source necessary equipment and cash for operations; serve as paymasters for ground-level operators; launder money	Accountants, lawyers, real-estate brokers, money changers, corrupt bank managers or other staff
Operations	Install illegal taps; staff taps and oversee loading; gather intelligence on oil, ship and state security-service movements	Local youths; former employees and contractors of the oil commission (alleged); small consortia of local elites; militant groups
Security	Stand sentry at tap point; secure the transport corridor; escort vessels in inland and coastal waters; gather intelligence; otherwise protect the network's "turf"	Local armed groups or "militants"; private security contractors; rank-and-file state security forces personnel (alleged)
Local transport	Provide the smaller ships, trucks and associated human resources needed to store stolen crude and/or carry it to ship-to-ship points in inland or coastal waters	Some local armed groups or "militants"; local and foreign shipping concerns; current and former politicians
Foreign transport	Provide the commercial-grade tankers and other vessels to carry stolen crude to destination points outside of Nigeria	Foreign shipping concerns and agents; some private commodities traders?
Sales	Broker sales of stolen parcels to foreign buyers; arrange for financing and shipment; remit profits to others in the network	Well-connected local intermediaries; some private commodities traders?
Low-level opportunists	Operate various types of protection/extortion rackets around theft rings to profit by exploiting oil thefts illegitimacy and/or by providing political cover	"Host" and "passage" communities, local elites, local armed groups and various types of youth gangs, rank-and-file security personnel

Source: Katsouris and Sayne (2013).

The more professional bunkering operations are highly armed and linked to foreigners. These include Moroccans, Venezuelans, Lebanese, Chinese and Russians, who own ships that load crude oil and deliver it for refining to Ghana, Cameroon and Côte d'Ivoire before transferring it to other markets (Alemika, 2013).

High-level involvement in Nigeria's oil theft has been a facet of the oil smuggling trade since the 1970s. Diverting oil through illicit channels permitted the then-military government to boost revenues and circumvent Organization of the Petroleum Exporting Countries (OPEC) restrictions. When the military junta turned into a democratic government, little was done to ensure more equitable division of resources; discontent grew substantially, along with greater opportunities for crime (Gboyega et al., 2011). Moreover, the Niger Delta has become a source of growing conflict, as oil theft has triggered what appears to be politically motivated violence and targeted attacks.

Considerable evidence exists of the ongoing association of senior levels of the government and military acting to facilitate the illicit trade in oil (Gillies, 2009). Protection unions operate along the illicit supply chain, taxing all actors engaged. Table 3.6 indicates the protection economy that has developed around the oil theft industry.

The role of neighbouring countries is also relevant. While some neighbouring countries, like Benin, have made seizures and investigated oil theft (Gillies, 2009), other states seem to be profiting from the spillover effects (Mayah, 2014). Fundamentally, only a few places in the world exist to offload tonnes of stolen fuel, and buyers with links to formal distribution operations are likely to be customers (UNODC, 2013b). Following money trails may help understand the flow's international dimensions.

Table 3.6. **Sample of alleged protection payments by oil thieves**

Item	Cost
Bribes to navy officers for tanker clearance	N 1.5 million (USD 9 50) for 500 000 litres (USD 3 per barrel)
"Security" payments at the tap point to: Local youth	N 700 000/week (USD 4 375)
Community government	N 1 million/week (USD 6 250)
	N 2 million/week (USD 12 500)

Note: N = Naira.

Source: Katsouris and Sayne (2013).

Stealing oil beyond the local level requires the participation of transnational organised-crime groups, who can ensure its transportation and sale once the oil leaves Nigeria's territorial waters (Gboyega et al., 2011). According to UNODC (2013b), the major international markets for stolen Nigerian oil are China, Democratic People's Republic of Korea, Israel and South Africa. International companies also play a role in the trade; the combination of tax write-offs and subsidies makes the level of theft a negligible expense (Katsouris and Sayne, 2013). In fact, whether companies are also involved in illicit trade is up for debate. In 2003, an investigation claimed that Nigeria could be losing as much as USD 600 million from illicit activities by international oil companies (Gboyega et al., 2011).

IFF implications and development impacts: Nigerian oil theft is largely cash-based, and bulk cash smuggling is common. For example, low-level employees may prefer to be paid in cash, while senior individuals may elect to purchase luxury goods or property through cash sales, taking advantage of these resources without resorting to the formal banking system. Nevertheless, it is assumed that the volume of illicit revenue raised through oil theft is far too high for the physical movement of currency to be the primary money-laundering vehicle. It is believed that the money-laundering process may be facilitated by bankers, lawyers and accountants, or may also use banks in other jurisdictions featuring less-robust anti-money laundering regimes (Katsouris and Sayne, 2013).

Beyond estimates of the scale of oil theft, its economic and developmental impact is not well researched. This knowledge gap can be filled by identifying transaction points and conducting investigations. For example, Chatham House reports that complex oil thefts require money to buy or rent vessels that move or store oil, as well as to pay intermediaries to launder the illicit proceeds. These are all entry points for a better investigation (Katsouris and Sayne, 2013).

Beyond Nigeria, the widespread practice of oil theft is also affecting neighbouring countries. In Benin, for example, a UN assessment mission found that smuggled fuel represented some 80% of all petroleum sold in the country, leading to the closure of many legal petrol stations (UNSC, 2012a). Furthermore, the failure to bring order and transparency to the oil industry in Nigeria is likely to dampen enthusiasm for further oil exploration in the region. Unless controls over the regional market in petroleum products can be reinforced, this will serve as a significant disincentive for investment (UNODC, 2013b).

Extractive industries

The ECOWAS region is endowed with significant mineral wealth, which has powered much of its economic growth over the past two decades. Ten of the 20 resource-rich African countries identified by the International Monetary Fund are located in West Africa. Some – such as Nigeria, Sierra Leone, Niger and Ghana – have been in the top tier of global economic performers; in each case, extractive minerals contributed 25% or more of their GDP. Yet that wealth has rarely translated into reduced poverty or inequality (Africa Progress Panel, 2013).

The negative relationship between extractive industries and illicit trade, crime, governance, conflict and development in West Africa is most clearly illustrated by the story of two of the region's most famous commodities: diamonds and gold. But this story is playing out again in relation to more recent, emerging industries, such as uranium in Niger or iron ore in Guinea.

Nature and scale of the flow: there are multiple ways to divert extractive resources and the revenue gained from them. These practices differ depending on the industry and country, making it difficult to estimate the magnitude and challenge of the trade. Some single data-point statistics provide a basis for evaluating the scale of the outflows:

- Estimates put the number of artisanal gold miners in Mali at between 100 000 and 200 000, producing around 4 tonnes of gold a year – 8% of national output – valued at USD 240 million (Africa Progress Panel, 2013). In Ghana, artisanal and small-scale miners are thought to number as many as 1 million today (Punam, Dabalen and Land, 2017).
- As of late 2013, the illicit trade in Ivorian diamonds was estimated at USD 12-23 million per year (UNSC, 2014a).
- In 2011, exports of mining products from Guinea reached USD 1.4 billion, representing 12% of GDP, but government mining revenues were just USD 48 million, or 0.4% of GDP (Africa Progress Panel, 2013).
- Between 50% and 90% of the diamond trade in Sierra Leone is lost through smuggling (Fanthorpe and Gabelle, 2013). At the same time, only one of the five major mining companies in Sierra Leone paid any corporate tax in 2011 (Africa Progress Panel, 2013).

The best data come from countries that were under embargo, and thus subject to international monitoring of their resource extraction. Côte d'Ivoire, until 2014 the subject of a UN diamond embargo, was shown to have an illicit trade almost equal to the USD 25 million in Ivorian diamonds exported legally before the embargo was imposed (UNSC, 2014a). The same document described an illegal river-dredging operation between Yamoussoukro and Seguela, in which 25 boats were reportedly extracting some USD 125 000 per month in gold (UNSC, 2014a). In Sierra Leone, anywhere from 50% to 90% of all diamonds mined by small-scale mining operations are not registered with local Kimberley Process offices, and many of these unregistered stones are smuggled out of the country (Vorrath, 2014). In Liberia, official gold exports over January-September 2013 stood at 416.5 kilogrammes, but actual production likely totalled around 3 000 kilogrammes, with most of the excess smuggled out of the country (UNSC, 2013a). An estimated 80% of Liberian gold miners operate without a licence, facilitating this large volume of illicit production (Vorrath, 2014).

The most vulnerable regions are those with the highest levels of mineral deposits. Sierra Leone was by far the largest diamond producer in West Africa in 2013, followed by Guinea, Ghana, Liberia and Togo (Kimberley Process, 2014). Production in Sierra Leone is concentrated in the districts of Kono (bordering Guinea), Kenema (bordering Liberia) and Bo. South-eastern Guinea and north-western Côte d'Ivoire are also active diamond-mining regions, with the area around the Ivorian city of Seguela notorious for smuggling (UNSC, 2014a). The mines are often located in isolated, heavily forested border regions with poor transportation links to national capitals, allowing smugglers to cross borders with ease. The same goes for gold: many diamond-mining regions are also active in the production and smuggling of gold.

Other mineral deposits can also be found across West Africa. The northern Niger regions of Zinder and Agadez are rich in uranium and oil, with concessions mined by French, Chinese and Canadian firms (International Crisis Group, 2013). The Simandou Mountains of Guinea contain one of the world's largest and highest-quality iron ore deposits (Samb, 2014). Iron ore in Simandou in Guinea, and petroleum projects in Liberia, could generate average annual revenues of USD 1.6 billion in each country; they represented 31% of GDP in Guinea and 147% of GDP in Liberia 2011 (Africa Progress Panel, 2013). Other major minerals mined in the region include bauxite, coal, rutile and coal.

Key actors: extractive-industry supply chains and related financial flows (both licit and illicit) involve a complex web and diverse set of actors. The forthcoming working paper on ASGM (OECD, forthcoming c) illustrates the complexity of these financial flows and the key actors involved. A number of criminal entrepreneurs have been identified in various UN monitoring reports for their role in smuggling gold and diamonds out of the region. West Africa is also allegedly a transit zone for diamonds from other parts of Africa; for example, diamond brokers in Monrovia have bought diamonds from Zimbabwe and the Central African Republic, and trafficked them to Liberia to evade Kimberley Process restrictions (UNSC, 2013a). Yet none of those who have been individually named have been prosecuted.

Some of the major players in this illicit economy also operate other legitimate businesses, which they use to launder their ill-gotten gains. The financier behind the trade in Ivorian diamonds from Seguela, for example, is the largest importer of motorcycles in northern Côte d'Ivoire, as well as managing trading companies specialising in agricultural products. Most of the gold illegally imported to Burkina Faso passes through the hands of an unnamed intermediary who owns a construction company that launders the proceeds of gold smuggling (UNSC, 2014a).

The issue of conflict minerals, where current or former combatants engage in predatory extraction, blurs the lines between political and criminal motivations for conflict. In 2014, the UN Panel of Experts on Liberia found that large numbers of former combatants were engaged in illicit mining (UNSC, 2014b). Similarly, a local commander for the Forces Nouvelles de Côte d'Ivoire, the main rebel group during the Ivorian Civil War and now a major political party, is allegedly smuggling both diamonds and gold out of the Seguela area. Gold operations are said to use labourers from Burkina Faso, which is also the final destination for the illicitly mined gold. The same commander also reportedly uses his connections to current and former security forces in the area to safeguard the cross-border illicit trade in Ivoirian diamonds (UNSC, 2014a).

To protect illicit resource flows, criminal groups co-opt the state. One of the reasons for the lack of consistent data on illicit mining is that relatively few arrests are made, owing to corruption in the criminal-justice sector (Vorrath, 2014).

IFF implications and development impacts: the Kimberley Process requires members to certify shipments of rough diamonds as "conflict-free" and prevent conflict diamonds from entering the legitimate trade. This necessitates licences for all related activities, from mining to exportation, reinforced by international sanctions (Kimberley Process, 2014). Liberia became a party to the Kimberley Process Certification Scheme in 2007, and Sierra Leone became a party in 2003 (Vorrath, 2014).

Initially, the Kimberley Process was heralded as a remarkable pact between the international community and the private sector to regulate the control of illicit diamonds along the supply chain. However, as open conflicts have been resolved and illicit activity has morphed into hybrid arrangements, the Kimberley Process has seen a significant reduction in efficacy. For example, it has been recently estimated that 50-90% of the diamond trade in Sierra Leone continues to be lost through smuggling (Fanthorpe and Gabelle, 2013).

Little is known about how the proceeds of illicit transactions are brought out of the region and laundered, perhaps due to the heavy emphasis on the trade in conflict minerals to the exclusion of other illicit flows and transactions. The trade in minerals can include diamond brokers and/or dealers, who engage miners and landowners, and allow illicit mining to occur on the land of which they are custodians. Legal licence holders may also use their licence to help legalise illicitly mined materials. National controls may also be avoided by sending diamonds to a factory, which polishes them to the point where they are no longer subject to Kimberley Process restrictions on rough diamonds before shipping them abroad, as occurred in Côte d'Ivoire (UNSC, 2013b). In many instances, no transactions appear to actually occur until the minerals leave West Africa. The UN Group of Experts on Côte d'Ivoire, for example, noted that "a portion of the Ivorian diamond production is sent to international trading, cutting and polishing centres directly through Abidjan and its international airport," and then sold in foreign markets (UNSC, 2013b).

A problematic consequence of diamond and gold smuggling is the loss of tax revenues for the region's governments. In 2009, for example, Sierra Leone passed the Mines and Minerals Act, which imposed export taxes of 5% on gold, 6.5% on precious stones and 15% on special stones with values exceeding USD 500 000. In the six months following the bill's passage, the country recorded zero official exports of gold or precious stones, while neighbouring Guinea and Liberia recorded increased exports. Between the Act's passage in 2009 and late 2014, only two special stones were exported from Sierra Leone (Vorrath, 2014). Desperate to recoup at least some of its lost tax revenue, the Government of Sierra Leone slashed the precious-stone tax from 6.5% to 3% in March 2011. In August 2012, it similarly cut the gold tax from 5% to 3% (Akam, 2012).

However, even if government revenues from the extractive industries were to be fully realised, there is little indication they would be put to work for development priorities. Resource-rich countries stand out as systematically underinvesting in social protection. Guinea and Niger both spend less than 0.5% of GDP on social protection, compared with a regional average of 2.5%. Nigeria also spends 1.5% of GDP on social protection, with limited coverage.

Flora and fauna

A large number of activities, including illegal fishing and logging, wildlife poaching, toxic-waste dumping and illicit trade in ozone-depleting chemicals, fall under the rubric of environmental crime. Although diverse, all these crimes either trade in environmental resources or critically harm the environment. These are rarely the most profitable forms of illicit trade, but they are often highly lucrative. Given their damage to local ecosystems –

and, concomitantly, local livelihoods – they also have a particularly detrimental impact on communities.

Nature and scale of the flow: illegal, unreported and unregulated (IUU) fishing and logging are the two most prevalent flora and fauna-related crimes in the West African context.

The West African Marine Eco-Region is one of the most bountiful fishing areas in the world. The fisheries sector employs approximately 1.5 million people, and comprises 15-17% of GDP and 25-30% of export revenues for the West African Marine Eco-Region (UNDP, 2012). The fishing industry earns countries like Mauritania, Senegal, Guinea, Guinea-Bissau, Ghana, Liberia and Sierra Leone an estimated USD 4.9 billion per year (World Bank, 2013). Estimates of the loss resulting from IUU range from USD 1.3 billion to USD 23.5 billion per year (Environmental Justice Foundation, 2012; Africa Progress Panel, 2014).

For IUU fishing, UNODC has identified two main trans-shipment hubs in West Africa: one in the eastern central Atlantic around Guinea and Guinea-Bissau, including Cabo Verde, Senegal and Gambia, and the other in the Gulf of Guinea, including Ghana, Togo, Benin and Nigeria (UNODC, 2011e). Illicit logging is concentrated in West Africa's coastal states, particularly Sierra Leone, Guinea-Bissau, Guinea and Liberia.

Environmental damage is occurring thanks to poor regulation in the logging sector and dumping of electronic waste. Between 2010 and 2012, the Liberian government sold one-quarter of the country's surface in logging permits. Without the capacity to properly oversee the rate of timber production, the country is estimated to have lost millions of dollars (Global Witness, 2013). Other countries in the region have struggled with the challenge; Guinea-Bissau's electoral campaigns in 2014 were allegedly funded by illicit logging revenue (IRIN News, 2014b).

While it has not reached the scale of Southern and Central Africa, wildlife poaching in West Africa is also a big concern. West Africa has become a hub for elephant-poaching. Abidjan's port has seen a number of major seizures (above 500 kilogrammes); Nigerians and Guinean networks are involved in the trade, while French-speaking West Africans supply ivory as far south as Angola. An investigation found an extensive operation by a Chinese syndicate active through Nigerian airports (Vira, Ewing and Miller, 2014).

The region's key species, such as the West African elephant population, have been poached to near-extinction, and the region is now becoming a transit hub for wildlife trafficking from East, Southern and Central Africa. Nigeria is a hub for trafficking of wildlife and wildlife products – particularly ivory, as it is well positioned to be resourced by multiple elephant-poaching hotspots, including Cameroon, Gabon, Republic of Congo and the Democratic Republic of the Congo (Vira, Ewing and Miller, 2014). Wildlife trafficking is now estimated to be the fifth most lucrative criminal activity, after the global trade in narcotics, arms, counterfeits and humans; it has more than doubled since 2007 (OECD, 2016).

Key actors: the illicit trade in flora and fauna in West Africa is facilitated by three types of actors: international corporations; national governments and state officials; and community-level local artisanal fishers and poachers.

International trawlers and fishers who exploit the weak regulatory capacity of West African coastal states are mainly responsible for illegal fishing (INTERPOL, 2014d). Between 1 January 2010 and 31 July 2012, the Environmental Justice Foundation received 252 reports of IUU fishing by industrial vessels within inshore areas. Commercial IUU fishers operate under flags of convenience or multiple identities to avoid detection.

Trans-shipment between trawlers is common, highlighting the degree of organisation in the illicit industry (Bondaroff, 2015). There is also evidence of collusion between local-level artisanal illegal fishers and international actors (INTERPOL, 2014d). The vessels engaging in industrial-scale illegal fishing in West Africa mainly come from Korea, China and other Asian countries (Lewerenz and Vorrath, 2015).

Lack of transparency and corruption in some coastal countries significantly enable IUU fishing. Information regarding the number of licences granted by governments and sold to foreign or nationally flagged commercial fishing boats is considered confidential. However, there are known cases of forged licences and complicity of senior-level officials allowing IUU (INTERPOL, 2014d; Lewerenz and Vorrath, 2015).

West African governments also have a long history of direct involvement in timber smuggling. In 2008, Sierra Leone imposed a ban on timber exports in response to indiscriminate exploitation of its forests by companies from China and other countries. Although domestic timber production went through a dizzying cycle of legalisation and prohibition in subsequent years, timber export remained illegal. At the same time, a strict timber ban in neighbouring Guinea drove smugglers across the border into Sierra Leone (Kavanagh, 2013). Allegations have surfaced that Chinese timber merchants, driven out of Guinea, entered Sierra Leone and relaunched their business ventures, paying locals with chainsaws rather than cash (Energy for Opportunity, 2012). A 2011 Al Jazeera investigation into illegal timber exportation in Sierra Leone found that local chieftains were felling trees and selling them indiscriminately. At the port in Freetown, police and customs officials looked the other way while containers with illegal logs bypassed cargo scanners. The investigation also found that the Office of the Vice President of Ghana had expedited the process of registering a timber-export company in exchange for the promise of nearly USD 100 000 in bribes; paperwork for the company was signed on the premises of the Ministry of Forestry (Samura, 2011). In June 2014, the President of Sierra Leone fired his chief of staff over accusations of improper mining deals and involvement in illegal timber exportation (Reuters, 2014).

IFF implications and development impacts: Despite the prevalence and seriousness of environmental crime, law-enforcement officials in the region give it relatively low priority. Table 3.7 shows the extent to which the region's customs officers perceive the illegal trade in wildlife as a threat. It is notable that West Africa has the lowest rate of respondents globally, and that scores indicate a relatively low degree of concern. The unregulated selling of concessions has been a revenue-generation strategy for a number of countries in the region. Low regulatory capacity, coupled with corruption, has also allowed firms to overexploit natural resources.

Table 3.7. **Customs officers' perception of the seriousness of illegal wildlife trade by region**

Region	Number of respondents	Response rate (%)	Poaching	Illegal export	Illegal import	Illegal transit
Middle East North Africa	10	58.8	3.1	3.3	3.3	2.7
West and Central Africa	10	43.5	3.1	2.9	2.6	2.4
East and Southern Asia	16	66.7	2.9	2.9	2.1	2.6
Americas and Caribbean	17	54.8	3.1	3.1	3.1	2.8
Europe	41	80.4	2.6	2.6	3.0	2.7
Asia Pacific	20	60.0	2.8	2.8	2.6	2.5

* 4: very serious; 3: somewhat serious; 2: not serious; 1: not an issue.

Source: World Customs Organization (2014).

Environmental crime challenges the region's ability to achieve its biodiversity goals and generate sustainable livelihoods. The proliferation of criminal networks means that local communities are more likely to engage in illicit trade, as legitimate opportunities are threatened. IUU fishing has a threefold impact on West Africa. First, it results in a direct financial loss to the economy. Second, it has an indirect – but more devastating – impact on communities that rely on fishing for sustenance. Third, IUU fishing has played a supporting role in other criminal operations: fishing vessels are a common method for trafficking drugs, and smuggling migrants and weapons, and are also used to perform acts of terrorism (UNODC, 2008; Platov, 2014).

The prioritisation framework applied to case studies

Table 3.8 shows how the analytical framework can be applied to three of the five case studies (to be published as separate Working Papers). Understanding the local market for a given criminal economy, the actors involved and what harm is caused can help policy makers to prioritise and tailor their intervention. The outcome highlights considerable differences between the impact of criminal economies and the response required, depending on where the IFF is earned and invested.

Table 3.8. **Applying an analytical framework to selected criminal economies**

	Cocaine traffic	Counterfeit goods	Artisanal gold mining
Where is the good sourced; and is there a local market?	**Externally:** cocaine is produced outside of the region, with only a small existing market for cocaine within the region. Trade is concentrated in a limited number of hands regionally; the main facilitators of the trade and beneficiaries of the IFFs generated are high-level public officials.	**Externally:** counterfeit goods are predominantly produced outside of the region, and yet enjoy a large local market. Depending on the goods, they sometimes compete with local products. Many actors engage in the movement and marketing of counterfeit goods. Depending on the product, the barriers to entry into the country are generally low.	**Locally:** gold is indigenous to the region. There is a sizeable local market for the good, which is used as a currency equivalent for local and cross-border trading.
Who are the actors involved?	**Latin American Cartels and high-level military and political officials.** Colombian or Latin American drug cartels work through high ranking and well-connected individuals, including key political and military personnel – individuals that control transport hubs or deploy military assets to protect trade.	**Entrepreneurs and corrupt officials/border guards.** The higher-level perpetrators of illicit trade in counterfeit or fake goods are "business executives" operating legitimately registered enterprises, corrupt officials and border guards. The producers and distributors of these goods are also important actors in the supply chain.	**Networks of local actors.** There is a diverse array of actors, from buyers to dealers, exporters and pre-financiers. Criminal groups co-opt state officials to protect the illicit flows, and former combatants are known to be involved in some ground-level operations. China and India lead the global demand for gold. Dubai and Switzerland are seen as leading the transit hubs.
Where are the IFFs earned and invested?	**Externally.** The bulk of the profits from the cocaine trade are realised externally to the region. The local IFFs are predominantly used to finance local operations, corruption and protection for those involved in the illegal trade. A small proportion of the locally realised flows are then laundered abroad.	**Externally.** The bulk of the IFFs are accrued outside of West Africa. Some profits are accrued by local importers and traders, but the majority are realised by producers. Locally accrued IFFs are often re-invested in local counterfeit operations, or make their way into the local economy.	**Locally.** The bulk of the IFFs accrued locally by the miners are invested locally in subsistence livelihoods or used in cross-border trade. A minority share of the IFFs produced along the value chain leaves the country through a limited number of mining companies or gold-dealing corporations.

Table 3.8. **Applying an analytical framework to selected criminal economies** (*continued*)

	Cocaine traffic	Counterfeit goods	Artisanal gold mining
Assessment of harm	The primary results from the cocaine trade include: – damage to health from drug use, which is still limited in West Africa – increased corruption through enrichment of local powerful elites, which may be colluding with criminals – violence resulting from increased armed protection and competition among groups that control the trade.	The primary harms from the counterfeits include: – negative impact on local industries – health and safety risks for consumers, e.g. from consuming counterfeit medication – loss of domestic revenue – increased corruption through enrichment of local powerful elites, which may be colluding with criminals.	The primary harms from artisanal scale mining include: – health and safety risks for artisanal miners, e.g. resulting from dangerous work practices or the use of toxic products – damage to the environment, resulting from the use of toxic products (e.g. mercury) – loss of government revenue – resourcing of local power brokers.
Implications of the response	Because of the limited local cocaine market (cocaine's penetration into social groups is commensurate with its high cost), responses should concentrate on their impact on the balance of power: – improved measures to seize the commodity prior to its transiting through West Africa (with the caveat that this will displace flows elsewhere) – targeted interventions (e.g. strengthening transparency and oversight to keep senior government officials from controlling the flow of drugs) – interventions focusing on breaking down the trafficking networks.	Counterfeit goods, though the object of limited attention from authorities in the region, are in heavy demand, mostly because of the lack of affordable legitimate alternatives. Responses should include: – for the goods most likely to cause physical harm (e.g. counterfeit medications), controlling the flows that cause the most harm to consumers and raising consumer awareness of the risks involved – providing viable market alternatives to consumers, possibly through government investment or subsidies – intervening with those producing and supplying the goods – addressing corruption, e.g. targeting relevant authorities with measures to improve transparency and oversight	Artisanal gold mining is more an informal than a criminal activity. Most of the value-chain benefits remain in the country, particularly in the community of the individuals involved. Responses should include: – mitigating harm to the environment – protecting those exposed, such as small-scale miners – shifting informal activity into the formal sector, both through legal and regulatory action, and providing incentives to the actors involved – creating/enforcing corporate regulation to address IFFs flowing outside of the region

Notes

1. The Nigerian Letter – also commonly referred to as "419 scams", named after section 419 of the Nigerian criminal code – was the first major type of cybercrime to emerge out of West Africa, with roots some analysts date back as far as the 1920s (Ellis, 2015). The Nigerian Letter is a scam that combines impersonation fraud with a variation of an advance-fee scheme in which the recipient is encouraged to send personal information to the scammer, which then uses it to defraud the victim of their personal assets. Perpetrators have been known to use personal information to impersonate the victim, draining bank accounts and credit-card balances. Some victims have been lured to Nigeria, where they are imprisoned against their will and lose large sums of money (Federal Bureau of Investigation, 2013). Second-generation cybercrime, including phishing, hacking and website cloning, is a significant evolution from crime based on unsolicited letters towards a more sophisticated internet-based criminal activity supported by document falsification, identity theft and money laundering (Shaw, Reitano and Hunter, 2014).

2. The risks remain low, as only five countries in West Africa (Cabo Verde, Nigeria, Senegal, Gambia and Ghana) are showing greater than 10% Internet prevalence.

3. Nigerian scammers are moving to Benin, but 40% of the individuals arrested in Ghana for cybercrime in 2008 were Nigerian (Boateng et al., 2011).

4. The Internet Crime Complaint Center in the United States reports that complaints originating in Nigeria only account for 0.08% of complaints received, ranking Nigeria 24th on the list of complaints received by country. However, Nigerian individuals are losing much greater sums of money (nearly USD 3 million) than other countries, ranking Nigerians 12th on the list of complaint losses by country (Internet Crime Complaint Center, 2014).

5. Algeria, Egypt, Libya, Morocco and Tunisia smoke 44% of all cigarettes consumed in Africa; an estimated 80% of all cigarettes smoked in Libya are thought to be illicit (UNODC, 2009).

6. For example, as highlighted in the forthcoming working paper on artisanal gold mining in Liberia and Ghana (OECD, forthcoming c), 34% of Ghana's gold in 2013 came from artisanal and small-scale gold mining activity (GHEITI, 2014), with over one million Ghanaians directly dependent on artisanal mining for their livelihoods (Africa Progress Panel, 2013).

7. Calculation at the annual inflation-adjusted price per barrel in 2012.

References

Abdelkader, G.K. and M. Zangaou (2012), *Wahaya: Domestic and Sexual Slavery in Niger*, Anti-Slavery International, London.

Africa Progress Panel (2014), *Africa Progress Panel Report 2014: Grain, Fish, Money*, Africa Progress Panel, Geneva.

Africa Progress Panel (2013), *Africa Progress Panel Report 2013: Equity in Extractives*, Africa Progress Panel, Geneva.

African Union (2014), *African Union Convention on Cyber Security and Personal Data Protection*, African Union, Addis Ababa.

Akam, S. (13 August 2012), "Sierra Leone plans gold tax cut to curb smuggling", Reuters, www.reuters.com/article/2012/08/13/sierraleone-gold-tax-idUSL6E8JDAKX20120813.

Akinyandenu, O. (2013), "Counterfeit drugs in Nigeria: A threat to public health", *African Journal of Pharmacy and Pharmacology*, Vol. 7/36, Open Access, pp. 2571-2576.

Alemika, E. (2013), *The Impact of Organised Crime on Governance in West Africa*, Friedrich-Ebert-Stiftung, Abuja.

Amnesty International (14 April 2015), "Nigeria: Abducted women and girls forced to join Boko Haram attacks", news blog, www.amnesty.org/en/latest/news/2015/04/nigeria-abducted-women-and-girls-forced-to- join-boko-haram-attacks.

Anders, H. (2014), *Identifying Sources: Small-calibre Ammunition in Côte d'Ivoire*, Small Arms Survey, Geneva.

Aning, K. & J. Pokoo (2014), "Understanding the nature and threats of drug trafficking to national and regional security in West Africa", *Stability: International Journal of Security and Development*, Vol. 3/1, Art. 8, http://doi.org/10.5334/sta.df.

Asare Kyei, A. (2013), "Falling on fertile grounds: The rise of drug-trafficking and the role of CSOs in West Africa", webpage, http://awoko.org/2013/02/12/falling-on-fertile-grounds-the-rise-of-drug-trafficking-and-the- role-of-csos-in-west-africa (accessed 22 February 2015).

Bah, A. (2004), "Micro-disarmament in West Africa: The ECOWAS moratorium on small arms and light weapons", *African Security Review*, Vol. 3/3, www.issafrica.org/pubs/asr/13No3/FBah.htm.

BAT (2010a), *Enhancing Supply Chain Security and Fighting the Illicit Trade in Tobacco Products*, British American Tobacco, London, www.bat.com/group/sites/uk__9d9kcy.nsf/vwPagesWebLive/DO933J8E/%24FILE/medMD9FZGBS.pdf?openelement.

BAT (2010b), *Illicit Trade: Nigeria*, British American Tobacco, London, www.batnigeria.com/group/sites/BAT_7YKM7R.nsf/vwPagesWebLive/DO7YLFT6?opendocumentandSKN=1.

Bavier, J. (2013), "West African cocaine, methamphetamine smuggling on the rise – U.N.", *Reuters*, http://uk.reuters.com/article/2013/02/25/uk-west-africa-drugs-idUKBRE91O14P20130225.

BBC (15 June 2015), "Profile: Mokhtar Belmokhtar", BBC News blog, www.bbc.com/news/world-africa- 21061480.

Bøås, M (2012), "Castles in the sand: Informal networks and power brokers in the northern Mali periphery", in Utas, M. (ed.), *African Conflicts and Informal Power: Big Men and Networks*, Zed Books, London and New York.

Boateng, R. et al. (2011), "Sakawa-cybercrime and criminality in Ghana", *Journal of Information Technology Impact*, Vol. 11/2, Regis University, Denver, pp. 85-100, www.jiti.com/v11/jiti.v11n2.085-100.pdf.

Bondaroff, T.P. (2015), *The IUU Fishing and Transnational Organised Crime Nexus: Illegal, Unregulated and Unreported Fishing as a Transnational Organized Crime*, Global Initiative against Transnational Organized Crime, Geneva.

Briscoe, I. (2014), *Crime after Jihad: Armed Groups, the State and Illicit Business in Post-Conflict Mali*, Clingendael, The Hague.

Callimachi, R. (24 July 2014), "Paying ransoms, Europe bankrolls Qaeda terror", *New York Times*, www.nytimes.com/2014/07/30/world/africa/ransoming-citizens-europe-becomes-al-qaedas-patron.html?_r=1.

Carlson, K. (2013), *Efficacy of Small Arms Control Measures and National Reporting: Learning from Africa*, Small Arms Survey, Geneva.

Chothia, F. (12 May 2014), "Will Nigeria's abducted schoolgirls ever be found?", BBC News blog, www.bbc.com/news/world-africa-27293418.

Control Risks (2016), "Response 2015 in Review", ControlRisks.com, https://www.controlrisks.com/~/media/Public%20Site/Files/Our%20Thinking/Infographics/20160426responseinfographic.pdf.

de Tessieres, S. (2012), *Enquête nationale sur les armes légères et de petit calibre en Côte d'Ivoire: Les défis du contrôle et de la lutte contre la violence armée avant la crise post-électorale*, Small Arms Survey, Geneva.

Dixon, R. (31 October 2013), "Scores die of starvation, thirst in Niger's desert on smuggling route", *Los Angeles Times*, http://articles.latimes.com/2013/oct/31/world/la-fg-wn-niger-migrants-20131031.

Dorn, N. and H. Van der Bunt (2012), *Bad Thoughts: Towards an Organised Crime Harm Assessment and Prioritisation Framework*, Erasmus School of Law, The Hague.

ECOWAS (2011), *Directive C/DIR 1/o8/11 on Fighting Cyber Crime within ECOWAS*, Sixty-Sixth Ordinary Session of the Council of Ministers, Economic Community of West African States, Abuja.

EJF (2012), *Pirate Fishing Exposed: The Fight against Illegal Fishing in West Africa and the EU*, Environmental Justice Foundation, London, http://ejfoundation.org/sites/default/files/public/Pirate%20Fishing%20Exposed.pdf.

Ellis, S. (2015), *A History of Nigerian Organised Crime*, African Studies Center, University of Leiden, Leiden.

Ellis, S. (2009), "West Africa's international drug trade", *African Affairs*, Vol. 108/431, Oxford Journals, London, pp. 171-196.

Energy for Opportunity (2012), *Timber and Fuelwood products in Sierra Leone: Current Dynamics and Issues*, Energy for Opportunity, Windsor.

European Union (2014a), "Combating transnational organised crime at sea: Background paper to a high level workshop held in Brussels 20-21 May 2014", European Union, Brussels.

European Union (2014b), "The EU launches a new project to fight falsified medications in developing countries", press release, http://europa.eu/rapid/press-release_IP-14-378_en.htm.

European Monitoring Centre for Drugs and Drug Addiction (2015), *Perspectives on Drugs: Opioid Trafficking Routes from Asia to Europe*, European Monitoring Centre for Drugs and Drug Addiction, Lisbon, www.emcdda.europa.eu/topics/pods/opioid-trafficking-routes#panel2.

Europol (2011), *EU Organised Crime Threat Assessment 2011*, Europol, The Hague.

Fanthorpe, R. and C. Gabelle (2013), *Political Economy of Extractives Governance in Sierra Leone*, World Bank, Washington, DC.

FATF (2013), *Terrorist Financing in West Africa*, Financial Action Task Force, Paris.

FATF (2012), *Illicit Tobacco Trade*, Financial Action Task Force, Paris.

FATF (2011a), *Organised Maritime Piracy and Related Kidnapping for Ransom*, Financial Action Task Force, Paris.

FATF (2011b), *Money Laundering Risks Arising from Trafficking in Human Beings and Smuggling of Migrants*, Financial Action Task Force, Paris.

Faucon, B. et al. (29 May 2013), "Africa's malarial battle: Fake drug pipeline undercuts progress", *Wall Street Journal*, www.wsj.com/articles/SB10001424127887324474004578444942841728204.

FBI (2013), *Common Fraud Schemes*, United States Federal Bureau of Investigation, Washington, DC.

Federal Trade Commission (20 October 2009), "MoneyGram to pay $18 million to settle FTC charges that it allowed its money transfer system to be used for fraud, Federal Trade Commission blog, www.ftc.gov/news-events/press-releases/2009/10/moneygram-pay-18-million-settle-ftc-charges-it-allowed-its-money.

Frontex (2015), *Monthly Analysis of Migratory Trends – May 2015*, Frontex, Warsaw, http://frontex.europa.eu/news/monthly-analysis-of-migratory-trends-may-2015-f02aLN.

Frontex (2014a), *FRAN Quarterly*, July-September 2014 (Q3), Frontex, Warsaw.

Frontex (30 September 2014b), "People smugglers: The latter day slave merchants", Frontex, Warsaw, http://frontex.europa.eu/feature-stories/people-smugglers-the-latter-day-slave-merchants-UArKn1.

Gaurvika, M. et al., (2012), "Poor quality anti-malarial drugs in southeast Asia and sub-Saharan Africa", *The Lancet*, June, Vol. 2/7, Elsevier, Amsterdam, pp. 488-496.

Gberie, L. (2015), *Crime, Violence and Politics: Drug Trafficking and Counternarcotics Policies in Mali and Guinea*, Brookings Press, Washington, DC.

Gboyega, A. et al. (2011), *Political Economy of the Petroleum Sector in Nigeria*, World Bank, Washington, DC.

GHEITI (2014), *GHEITI Report for 2012 and 2013*, Ghana Extractive Industries' Transparency Initiative, Accra.

GIABA (2013), *The Nexus between Small Arms and Light Weapons and Money Laundering and Terrorist Financing in West Africa*, Inter-Governmental Action Group against Money Laundering in West Africa, Dakar.

GIABA (2010), *Threat Assessment of Money Laundering and Terrorist Financing in West Africa*, Inter-Governmental Action Group against Money Laundering in West Africa, Dakar.

Gillies, A. (2009), *Reforming Corruption out of Nigerian Oil?, Part One: Mapping Corruption Risks in Oil Sector Governance*, Anti-Corruption Resource Centre, Oslo.

Global Initiative (February 2016), *Trails of Insecurity: Illicit Migration as a Source of Threat Financing and Criminal Resourcing in Africa*, Conference report, The Global Initiative against Transnational Organized Crime, Addis Abeba.

Global Initiative (2014a), *Organized Crime as Cross-Cutting Threat to Sustainable Development: Measuring and Monitoring Transnational Organized Crime within the Framework of Sustainable Development for the Post-2015 Development Agenda*, Global Initiative against Transnational Organized Crime, Geneva.

Global Initiative (2014b), *Bittersweet Easter: Child Trafficking in the Chocolate Industry*, The Global Initiative against Transnational Organized Crime, Analyzing Organized Crime blog, www.globalinitiative.net/bittersweet-easter.

Global Witness (2013), *Avoiding the Riptide: Liberia Must Enforce its Forest Laws to Prevent a New Wave of Illegal and Destructive Logging Contracts*, June, Global Witness, London, twww.globalwitness.org/en-gb/archive/liberiaCFMA.

Golub, S.S. (2012), "Entrepot trade and smuggling in West Africa: Benin, Togo and Nigeria", *The World Economy*, Swarthmore.

HLP (2015), *Track it, Stop it, Get it: Illicit Financial Flows from Africa*, High Level Panel on Illicit Financial Flows from Africa, African Union/ECA Conference of Ministers, Addis Ababa.

Howell, S. and A. Atta-Asamoah (2015), "West Africa and the transnational trade in illegal drugs: Physical properties, policing and power", *Africa Review*, Vol. 7/1, National Media Group, pp. 1-14.

IC3 (2014), *2014 IC3 Annual Report*, Internet Crime Complaint Center, Federal Bureau of Investigation, Washington, DC, www.ic3.gov/media/annualreport/2014_IC3Report.pdf.

ICG (2013), *Niger: Another Weak Link in the Sahel?*, International Crisis Group, Brussels.

IEA (2014), *Africa Energy Outlook Special Report: A Focus on Energy Prospects in Sub-Saharan Africa*, IEA/OECD Publishing, Paris.

Imperial Tobacco (2014), "Combatting illicit trade in Mali", webpage, www.imperial-tobacco.com/index.asp?page=78andnewscategory=andyear=2014andnewsid=2002 (accessed 2 March 2015).

International Maritime Bureau (2015), *Piracy and Armed Robbery against Ships: Report for the Period 1 January-31 December 2014*, International Chamber of Commerce, London.

International Maritime Bureau (2014), *Live Piracy Map 2014*, IMB Piracy Reporting Centre, International Chamber of Commerce, London, https://icc-ccs.org/piracy-reporting-centre/live-piracy-map/piracy-map-2014 (accessed 22 February 2015).

INTERPOL (2014a), "Forced child labour", webpage, www.interpol.int/Crime-areas/Trafficking-in-human-beings/Operations/Forced-child-labour (accessed 22 February 2015).

INTERPOL (2014b), *Pharmaceutical Crime and Organised Criminal Groups*, INTERPOL, Lyon.

INTERPOL (2014c), *Motor Vehicle Crime in a Global Perspective*, INTERPOL, Lyon.

INTERPOL (2014d), *Study on Fisheries Crime in the West Africa Coastal Region*, INTERPOL, Lyon.

IOM (2011), *International Migration Annual Review 2010/11*, International Organization for Migration, Geneva.

IOM and UNHCR (2011), *Protecting Refugees and Other Persons on the Move in the ECOWAS Space,* International Organization for Migration and UN High Commissioner for Refugees, Geneva.

IRIN News (21 February 2014a), "Arms smuggling to Boko Haram threatens Cameroon", IRIN, www.irinnews.org/report/99682/arms-smuggling-to-boko-haram-threatens-cameroon.

IRIN News (22 July 2014b), "Rosewood plunder in Guinea-Bissau", IRIN, www.irinnews.org/report/100387/rosewood-plunder-in-guinea-bissau.

ITU (2016), *ITU: ICT Statistics* (database), www.itu.int/en/ITU-D/Statistics/Pages/stat/default.aspx (accessed 4 April 2015).

Jenkins, B.M. (29 January 2013), "The motivations behind the Amenas terrorist attack", The Rand Blog, www.rand.org/blog/2013/01/the-motivations-behind-the-amenas-terrorist-attack.html.

JLT Group (2012), *Kidnapping and Ransom Bulletin*, October, JLT Specialty Limited, London, www.jltgroup.com/content/UK/risk_and_insurance/Newsletter/265861_KR_Bulletin_Africa_Final_1.pdf.

Kamal-Deen, A. (2015), "The anatomy of Gulf of Guinea piracy", *Naval War College Review*, Vol. 68/1, Winter, Naval War College, Newport, pp. 93-118, www.usnwc.edu/getattachment/e95feaa7-8883-4008-b49b-175783f25e43/The-Anatomy-of-Gulf-of-Guinea-Piracy.aspx.

Katsouris, C. and A. Sayne (2013), *Nigeria's Criminal Crude: International Options to Combat the Export of Stolen Oil*, Chatham House, London.

Kavanagh, C. (2013), *Getting Smart and Scaling up: Responding to the impact of Organised Crime on Governance in Developing Countries*, Centre for International Cooperation, New York.

Kimberley Process (2014), *Annual Global Summary 2014*, Kimberley Process, http://kimberlyprocess.com.

Kimberley Process (2013), "About", webpage, www.kimberleyprocess.com/en/about (accessed 21 December 2015).

Kleist, N. (2011), *Europe Fighting Irregular Migration - Consequences for West African Mobility*, Danish Institute for International Studies, Stockholm.

Kobo, K. (28 August 2014), "Cracking down on cybercrime in Ivory Coast", Al Jazeera, www.aljazeera.com/news/africa/2014/08/cracking-down-cybercrime-ivory-coast-20148279503515697.html.

Lacher, W. (2013), "Challenging the myth of the drug-terror nexus in the Sahel", background paper, No. 4, West Africa Commission on Drugs, Geneva, www.wacommissionondrugs.org/wp-content/uploads/2013/09/Challenging-the-Myth-of-the-Drug-Terror-Nexus-in-the-Sahel-Wolfram-Lacher.pdf.

Lacher, W. (2012), *Organised Crime and Conflict in the Sahel-Sahara Region*, Carnegie Endowment for International Peace, Washington, DC.

Lewerenz, C. and J. Vorrath (2015), *Illegal Fishing and Maritime Security: Towards a Land and Sea based Response to Threats in West Africa*, German Institute for International and Security Affairs, Berlin.

Mackey, T.K. and B.A. Liang (2013), "Improving global health governance to combat counterfeit medicines: A proposal for a UNODC-WHO-Interpol trilateral mechanism", *BMC Medicine*, Vol. 11/233, University of California, San Diego.

Madeira, L. et al. (2011), *The International Cocaine Trade in Guinea-Bissau: Current Trends and Risks*, Norwegian Peacebuilding Centre, Oslo.

Maertens, F. and A.P. de Andres (2009), "West Africa: trafficking central station?" *NATO Review*, July, www.nato.int/docu/review/2009/Organized_Crime/Transnational_Trafficking_West_Africa/EN/index.htm.

Mayah, E. (24 May 2014), "Togo triangle: Where stolen Nigerian crude is sold", The Niche Online.

McLaughlin, K. (5 June 2014), "New wave of drug-resistant malaria threatens millions", *The Guardian*, www.theguardian.com/society/2014/jun/05/new-wave-drug-resistant-malaria-burma.

Newton, P.N. (2008), "A collaborative epidemiological investigation into the criminal fake artesunate trade in SouthEast Asia", *Plos Medicine*, 12 February.

NPR (31 July 2014), *Kidnapping Is A Lucrative Business For Al-Qaida, Documents Show*, National Public Radio, www.npr.org/templates/transcript/transcript.php?storyId=336847324.

Oceans Beyond Piracy (2014), *The State of Maritime Piracy Report 2014*, One Earth Future Foundation, Denver.

OECD (forthcoming a), "Case study: Illicit narcotics transiting West Africa", OECD Publishing, Paris.

OECD (forthcoming b), "Case study: Illicit trade in counterfeit and substandard goods in Ghana", OECD Publishing, Paris.

OECD (forthcoming c), "Case study: The artisanal and small-scale gold mining sector", OECD Publishing, Paris.

OECD (2016), *Illicit Trade: Converging Criminal Networks*, OECD Publishing, Paris, http://dx.doi.org/10.1787/9789264251847-en.

OECD (2015), *Development Aid at a Glance: 2015*, OECD, Paris, www.oecd.org/dac/financing-sustainable-development/development-finance-data/aid-at-a-glance.htm.

OECD (2014), *Illicit Financial Flows from Developing Countries: Measuring OECD Responses*, OECD Publishing, Paris, http://dx.doi.org/10.1787/9789264203501-en.

OECD (2013), *Settlement, Market and Food Security*, OECD Publishing, Paris, http://dx.doi.org/10.1787/9789264187443-en.

Ogala, E. (21 March 2014), "Investigation: How multi-billion naira illicit tobacco trade thrives in Nigeria, putting millions at risk", *Premium Times*, www.premiumtimesng.com/news/157129-how-multibillion-naira-illicit-tobacco-trade-thrives-in-nigeria.html.

Ogisi, M. (5 October 2011), "Fake medicines common in many sub-Saharan African countries", Gallup Poll blog, www.gallup.com/poll/149942/%20Fake-Medicine-Common-Sub-Saharan-African-Countries.aspx.

Ohene-Asare, S. et al. (2014), *Trafficking of Small Arms and Light Weapons (SALW) in West Africa: Routes and Illegal Arms Caches between Ghana, Togo, Benin and Nigeria*, Friedrich-Ebert-Stiftung, Abuja.

Onuoha, F.C. (8 September 2013), *Porous Borders and Boko Haram's Small Arms Smuggling Operations in Nigeria*, Al-Jazeera Centre for Studies blog, http://studies.aljazeera.net/en/reports/2013/09/201398104245877469.htm.

O'Regan, D. and P. Thompson (2013), *Advancing Stability and Reconciliation in Guinea-Bissau: Lessons from Africa's First Narco-state*, Africa Center for Strategic Studies, Washington, DC.

Osinowo, A.A. (2015), *Combating Piracy in the Gulf of Guinea*, Africa Center for Strategic Studies, Washington, DC.

Oxfam (2012), *Embargoed States Importing Arms (2001-10)*, Oxfam, London.

Oxford Analytica (2013), *West Africa Criminal Networks Adapt and Shift East*, Oxford Analytica, Oxford, www.oxan.com.

Platov, V. (18 April 2014), "Transnational organised crime in the fishing industry", New Eastern Outlook blog, http://journal-neo.org/2014/04/18/rus-transnatsional-naya-organizovannaya-prestupnost-v-sfere-ry-bolovnogo- promy-sla.

Polgreen, L. (6 February 2009), "84 children are killed by medicine in Nigeria", *New York Times*, www.nytimes.com/2009/02/07/world/africa/07nigeria.html.

Punam C., A. Dabalen and B. Land (2017), *Mining in Africa: Are Local Communities Better Off?*, Africa Development Forum, World Bank, Washington, DC.

Refworld (2014), *Nigeria: Kidnapping for Ransom, including Frequency, Profile of Victims and Kidnappers; Response by Authorities (2013-July 2014)*, Immigration and Refugee Board of Canada, 31 July 2014, www.refworld.org/docid/546dc1724.html.

Reitano, T. and M. Shaw (2015), *Fixing a Fractured State? Breaking the Cycles of Crime, Corruption and Conflict in Mali and the Sahel*, Global Initiative against Transnational Organized Crime, Geneva.

Reitano, T. and P. Tinti (2015), *Survive and Advance: The Economics of Smuggling Migrants and Refugees into Europe*, Institute for Security Studies, Pretoria.

Reitano, T., L. Adal and M. Shaw (2014), *Smuggled Futures: The Dangerous Path of a Migrant from Africa to Europe*, Global Initiative against Transnational Organized Crime, Geneva.

Reuters (10 June 2014), "Sierra Leone president sacks chief of staff over timber, mine deals", Reuters, http://news.yahoo.com/sierra-leone-president-sacks-chief-staff-over-timber-080920933.html.

Revenue Watch Institute (2013), *The 2013 Resource Governance Index*, Revenue Watch Institute, New York.

Samb, S. (5 August 2014), "Guinea's Simandou iron ore trove: huge potential for the hugely patient", Reuters, www.reuters.com/article/2014/08/05/guinea-mining-simandou-idUSL6N0QB5LD20140805.

Samura, S. (26 November 2011), "Timber!", Al Jazeera.

Shaw, M. (2015), "Drug trafficking in Guinea-Bissau 1998-2014: The evolution of an elite protection network", *Journal of Modern African Studies*, Vol. 53/3, Cambridge University Press, pp. 339-364.

Shaw, M. and F. Mangan (2014), *Illicit Trafficking and Libya's Transition*, United States Institute for Peace, Washington, DC.

Shaw, M. and T. Reitano (2014), *The Political Economy of Trafficking and Trade in the Sahara: Instability and Opportunities*, World Bank, Washington, DC.

Shaw, M., T. Reitano and M. Hunter (2014), *Comprehensive Assessment of Drug Trafficking and Organised Crime in West and Central Africa*, African Union, Addis Ababa.

Shelley, L. (2014), *Human Smuggling and Trafficking into Europe: A Comparative Perspective*, Migration Policy Institute, Washington, DC.

Shelley, L. and S. Melzer (2008), "The nexus of organised crime and terrorism: Two case studies in cigarette smuggling", *International Journal of Comparative and Applied Criminal Science*, Vol. 32/1, Taylor and Francis Online, pp. 43-63.

Small Arms Survey (2013), *Rebel Forces in Northern Mali: Documented Weapons, Ammunition and Related Material*, Small Arms Survey, London and Geneva.

Stewart, P. and L. Wroughton (1 July 2014), "How Boko Haram is beating U.S. efforts to choke its financing", *Reuters*, www.reuters.com/article/2014/07/01/us-usa-nigeria-bokoharam-insight-idUSKBN0F636920140701.

Stewart, S. (2010), "A look at kidnapping through the lens of protective intelligence", Stratefor Security Weekly blog, www.stratfor.com/weekly/20100519_look_kidnapping_through_lens_protective_intelligence.

The Economist (14 September 2013), "Kidnapping in Nigeria: A holy mess", *The Economist*, www.economist.com/news/middle-east-and-africa/21586355-kidnapping-nigeria-out-hand-holy-mess.

UltraScan (2014), *419 Scams*, UltraScan AGI, Amsterdam.

UN.GIFT (2008), *Human Trafficking: An Overview*, United Nations, Vienna.

UNCTAD (31 March 2014), "West African countries helped to harmonize cyber laws at UNCTAD workshop in Ghana", All News blog, United Nations Conference on Trade and Development, Geneva, http://unctad.org/en/pages/newsdetails.aspx?OriginalVersionID=714.

UNDP (2012), *Strengthening Governance and Management of Marine Resources in West Africa*, United Nations Development Programme, New York.

UNODC (2014a), *World Drug Report 2014*, United Nations Office on Drugs and Crime, Vienna.

UNODC (2014b), *2014 Global Synthetic Drugs Assessment*, United Nations Office on Drugs and Crime, Vienna.

UNODC (2014c), *The Globalization of Crime: A Transnational Organised Crime Threat Assessment*, United Nations Office on Drugs and Crime, Vienna.

UNODC (2014d), *Global Report on Trafficking in Persons 2014*, United Nations Office on Drugs and Crime, Vienna.

UNODC (2013a), *World Drug Report 2013*, United Nations Office on Drugs and Crime, Vienna.

UNODC (2013b), *Transnational Organised Crime in West Africa: A Threat Assessment*, United Nations Office on Drugs and Crime, Vienna.

UNODC (2013c), *Comprehensive Study on Cybercrime*, United Nations Office on Drugs and Crime, Vienna.

UNODC (2012a), *World Drug Report 2012*, United Nations Office on Drugs and Crime, Vienna.

UNODC (2012b), *Global Report on Trafficking in Persons 2012*, United Nations Office on Drugs and Crime, Vienna.

UNODC (2011a), *Estimating Illicit Flows from Drug Trafficking and other forms of Transnational Organised Crime*, United Nations Office on Drugs and Crime, Vienna.

UNODC (2011b), *World Drug Report 2011*, United Nations Office on Drugs and Crime, Vienna.

UNODC (2011c), *The Transatlantic Cocaine Market*, United Nations Office on Drugs and Crime, Vienna.

UNODC (2011d), *The Role of Organised Crime in Smuggling Migrants from Africa to Europe*, United Nations Office on Drugs and Crime, Vienna.

UNODC (2011e), *Transnational Organised Crime in the Fishing Industry*, United Nations Office on Drugs and Crime, Vienna.

UNODC (2009), *Transnational Trafficking and the Rule of Law in West Africa: A Threat Assessment*, United Nations Office on Drugs and Crime, Vienna.

UNODC (2008), *Drug Trafficking as a Security Threat in West Africa*, United Nations Office on Drugs and Crime, Vienna.

UNSC (2014a), "Letter dated 14 April 2014 from the Vice-Chair of the Security Council Committee established pursuant to Resolution 1572 (2204) concerning Côte d'Ivoire address to the President of the Security Council (S/2014/266)", United Nations Security Council, New York.

UNSC (2014b), *Midterm Report of the Panel of Experts on Liberia submitted pursuant to paragraph 5(b) of Security Council Resolution 2128 (2013) (S/2014/363)*, United Nations Security Council, New York.

UNSC (2014c), *Security Council Adopts Resolution 2133 (2014), Calling upon States to Keep Ransom Payments, Political Concessions from Benefiting Terrorists*, United Nations Security Council, New York.

UNSC (2013a), "Letter dated 19 November 2013 from the Chair of the Security Council Committee established pursuant to Resolution 1521 (2003) concerning Liberia, addressed to the President of the Security Council (S/2103/683)", United Nations Security Council, New York.

UNSC (2013b), "Letter dated 11 October 2013 from the Chair of the Security Council Committee established pursuant to resolution 1572 (2004) concerning Côte d'Ivoire addressed to the President of the Security Council (S/2013/605)", United Nations Security Council, New York.

UNSC (2012a), *Report of the United Nations Assessment Mission on Piracy in the Gulf of Guinea (7 to 24 November 2011) (S/2012/45)*, United Nations Security Council, New York.

UNSC (2012b), "Letter dated 15 October 2012 from the Chair of the Security Council Committee established pursuant to resolution 1572 (2004) concerning Côte d'Ivoire addressed to the President of the Security Council (S/2012/766)", United Nations Security Council, New York.

US Department of State (2014), *Trafficking in Persons Report 2014*, United States Department of State, Washington, DC.

US-ICE (2014), "Nigerian national sentenced in scheme to ship stolen vehicles to West Africa", United States Immigration and Customs Enforcement, News Release, 8 June 2014, www.ice.gov/news/releases/nigerian- national-sentenced-scheme-ship-stolen-vehicles-west-africa.

Vira, V., T. Ewing and J. Miller (2014), *Out of Africa: Mapping the Global Trade in Illicit Elephant Ivory*, C4DS and Born Free USA, Washington, DC, www.wwf.se/source.php/1578610/out%20of%20africa.pdf.

Vorrath, J. (2014), *From War to Illicit Economies: Organised Crime and State Building in Liberia and Sierra Leone*, Stiftung Wissenschaft und Politik, Berlin.

WACD (2014), *Not Just in Transit: Drugs, the State and Society in West Africa*, West Africa Commission on Drugs, Geneva.

WCO (2014), *A Survey of Customs Administration Perceptions on Illegal Wildlife Trade*, World Customs Organization, Geneva.

WCO (2013), *Illicit Trade Report 2013*, World Customs Organization, Brussels.

WCO (2010), *Customs and Tobacco Report 2009*, World Customs Organization, Brussels.

WHO (2014), *World Malaria Report 2014*, World Health Organization, Geneva.

WHO (2010), "Growing threat from counterfeit medicines", *Bulletin*, World Health Organization, Geneva, www.who.int/bulletin/volumes/88/4/10-020410/en.

Wilson, K. (29 June 2009), *Terrorism and Tobacco,* International Consortium of Investigative Journalists, www.icij.org/project/tobacco-underground/terrorism-and-tobacco.

World Bank (2014a), *GDP per capita (current USD)* (database), http://data.worldbank.org/indicator/NY.GDP.PCAP.CD?page=1 (accessed 30 December 2014).

World Bank (2014b), *World Development Indicators 2014*, World Bank, Washington, DC.

World Bank (2013), *World Bank, West Africa: Fishing Communities Restore Health to Ocean Habitats*, World Bank, Washington, DC.

Interviews

SEN-GIABA-130515: Multiple senior research and policy officers, GIABA, in person, 13 May 2015.

UK-Gov-LE-220615: Multiple, National Crime Agency Officers, United Kingdom, interviewed in person, 22 June 2015.

VIE-UNODC-290515: Senior UNODC Official, by Skype, 29 May 2015.

Chapter 4.

Conclusions and recommendations

Based on an analysis of illicit financial flows (IFFs), this report establishes an analytical framework for understanding the harm that can be generated by criminal economies in order to guide and prioritise responses, both by the states in the region and the international community. These conclusions were drawn from an analysis of 13 forms of illicit or criminal economies operating in the region, organised by a typology distinguishing between illegal activities, the illicit exploitation or commodification of natural-resource assets, and the illicit trade in normally legal goods. This final chapter concludes with several observations and recommendations that draw on commonalities, but are also targeted at the development, finance and trade, and security and justice sectors. It draws on the report's findings to determine a way for state and non-state actors to plan and co-ordinate their responses.

Introduction

Illicit financial flows (IFFs), defined as "money illegally earned, transferred or used" (United Nations Economic Commission for Africa [ECA], 2013), are increasingly understood as a threat to sustainable development and a shared global challenge. They constrain economic growth and undermine investment, depriving governments of the financial resources that might otherwise be invested in public goods, such as health, education or infrastructure.

IFFs carry a high price and can be linked to dangerous illicit or criminal activities, such as human trafficking, drug trafficking and conflict minerals. IFFs are particularly prevalent and damaging in the context of fragile and transition countries, where they contribute to vicious cycles of low development, instability and conflict by further weakening fragile public institutions and empowering those who operate outside of the law.

This report identified 13 forms of illicit or criminal economies operating in the region, organising them in a typology that clearly distinguished illegal activities from the illicit exploitation or commodification of natural-resource assets, and the illicit trade in normally legal goods.

Governments' resilience and capacity to counter criminal economies and prevent IFFs reflect the resources available to them, and the political will to do so. Yet because of West Africa's porous borders, the large areas where the state has little impact or control, and the predominantly informal economies governing domestic, regional and international transactions, it is difficult to see how conventional tools designed to mitigate IFFs (such as those focusing on law enforcement) can be effective in the region. In all states, countering and containing the most pervasive illicit trades is a struggle. In West Africa, the task is even more challenging; it is further complicated by the fact that these economies often provide basic livelihoods to populations living in affected areas. Responding to this complex set of problems requires interventions that directly tackle criminal networks and mitigate harms, while simultaneously working to alleviate the development conditions that might give rise to IFFs. The way illicit and criminal activities function, and the means by which their IFFs are laundered, are also fluid: they change in response to the environment, opportunity and both global and local market drivers, and no single entity or organisation will succeed in addressing IFFs by working in isolation.

Main findings and conclusions

The persistence and agility of criminal economies is a product of increasingly interdependent global markets. Resources are finite, and the challenges of reducing the occurrence and impact of IFFs are many, particularly in fragile-state contexts, which characterise several of the countries in the West African region. Some illicit markets are clearly more damaging than others. If policy makers can understand how criminal markets work, the way in which they interact with local communities and local forces, and how they garner profit, they can prioritise their interventions and learn to mitigate those activities that do the most damage.

Despite the diversity of criminal economies considered in this report, a number of common conclusions can be drawn. These relate in particular to the enabling conditions in the West African region that allow individuals to undertake these activities without significant resistance. As is the case globally, criminal networks operating in West Africa are able to move flexibly between markets and commodities with relative impunity, generating rents that will enable them to further perpetuate the conditions they need to thrive: corrupt officials buying legitimacy and support from local communities.

The licit and illicit are interwoven

It is often hard to draw the line at where livelihoods end and criminality begins; not all that happens informally should be construed as illegal. Yet, distinguishing between the licit and the illicit in West Africa is not straightforward, for two reasons. First, given the expansive nature of the informal economy (estimated at 50-80% region wide), most West Africans generate their livelihoods outside of the formal trade and regulatory framework (United Nations Economic Commission for Africa [ECA], 2012). Whole borderland communities rely on informal cross-border trade of commodities, the vast majority of which are food products: for example, a breakdown of the multi-million dollar weekly value of cross-border smuggling from Algeria to Mali estimated that over 85% of commodities were basic food items like flour, pasta or milk powder (OECD/Sahel and West Africa Club Secretariat [SWAC], 2014). As the forthcoming study on gold issued from artisanal and small-scale gold mining (AGSM) demonstrates, the incomes generated by artisanal miners through this illicit activity are economic mainstays for the local economy (OECD, forthcoming a). With few viable opportunities for livelihoods within the formal economy, these are subsistence forms of trade and industry. Activities like commodity smuggling – or even human smuggling – are not necessarily stigmatised as criminal behaviour,[1] and a range of local services may develop in tandem with them to optimise the potential for downstream benefits. For example, towns on dominant migrant or drug routes have developed a host of services, including providing accommodation, food and armed security for hire. This amplifies the benefits of illicit trade and creates economic dependency on the part of the community.

Criminal economies and their links to corruption

The criminal economies presented in this report reflect that politics, governance and illicit activity are often interconnected, and public officials often wear multiple hats – as public officials performing their public role, but also as private individuals connected to local, community or family networks, and sometimes linked to criminal or illegal activity and cross-border trade. Loose lines and affiliations cause the licit and illicit to become blurred. At the same time, the size of the unregulated financial sector, the weak capacity of customs and borders authorities, and low levels of political commitment to change the status quo enable these activities to persist without penalty or censure. Key figures in business and government can serve as pivotal nodes in the networks that perpetuate criminal behaviour, initiating or organising transactions domestically and with international markets, protecting flows from seizure and network members from prosecution, and laundering money through legitimate business or international trade. This model is best analysed and understood in the extractive sector, but it applies equally to the trade in consumer goods and illegal goods (such as illicit drugs).

In the higher ranks, those engaged in the criminal economies are free to parlay their IFFs into political power or economic leverage. At the lower levels, corruption may serve as a means of livelihood. The payment of a bribe is perceived as a right of office in a system where civil service salaries are low and often irregular. It is an expected cost of doing business for individuals engaged in both licit and illicit activity, and payments typically increase according to rank. In this manner, both governance and politics become invested in protecting illicit flows. It is said the practice is so widespread and pervasive that it can be better defined as an alternative system of governance, rather than as corruption (Chayes, 2015). Nevertheless, it is an alternative system that reduces the development prospects and life chances of the society's poorest and most vulnerable (Burgis, 2015).

Extortion or protection taxes and financial exclusion strengthen criminal economies

The ability to levy taxes on trade, both licit and illicit, is increasingly falling outside of the purview of West African central states. As the forthcoming study on drug trafficking demonstrates, charging for protection is a strategy of criminal groups involved in drug trafficking and other forms of illegal behaviour (OECD, forthcoming b). The case study on the financing of Al Qaeda in the Islamic Maghreb showed that terrorist groups active in West Africa are able to garner income from taxing or extorting the communities in which they operate, including in relation to legitimate economic activities. Money flows to local powerbrokers or terrorist groups, as it would (should) to the state; in this environment, protection becomes a commodity in itself, and violence plays a pivotal role in the fight for control (Shaw, 2016). The bribes paid to low-level officials are ultimately an additional tax levied on the people, diverted from the coffers of the treasury. The large size of the informal economy, and the blurred lines between legitimate and illegitimate economic activity, make addressing this resource diversion particularly challenging.

Financial exclusion as a driver of IFFs

A central factor enabling criminal economies and IFFs to thrive in West Africa are the region's low levels of financial inclusion. Access to the formal banking system is out of reach of the vast majority of ordinary people. The principal means for remittance exchange and international transactions, the money transfer operators (MTOs), are prohibitively expensive. This has created a paradigm in which the majority of financial transactions are conducted in cash and the *hawala*[2] system is favoured for longer-distance or cross-border payments. As a result, significant volumes of transactions are outside of government regulators' reach, and cannot be measured for the purposes of international trade.

The consequences of so much economic activity falling outside of the formal system are manifold. First, the ubiquity of informal cash-transfer systems increases the risks of money laundering and terrorist financing. It also impedes the important benefits derived from access to banking and savings products, including the empowerment of women, increased productive investment and consumption, raised productivity and incomes, and increased expenditures on preventive health (World Bank, 2014).

A large number of law-enforcement professionals and financial regulators were interviewed for this study, both within the region and externally; all recognised the inherent challenge of preventing IFFs in a context of strong *hawala* systems (SEN-GIABA-130515; NIG-Gov-LE-220915; UK-Gov-LE- 220615; USA-Gov-LE-120515; WA-EU-080515; WA-EUSec-120515). It appears that the implementation of anti-money laundering/countering the financing of terrorism (AML/CFT) regulations, along with other factors, has led banks to adopt a more conservative position to limit their risk exposure in developing countries. This process, referred to as "de-risking", further affects the prospects of financial inclusion for those on the margins of the economy. For example, the AGSM case study highlights that access to credit may have allowed informal miners to afford licenses, buy equipment and shift into more formal employment (OECD, forthcoming a).

Most West African countries set a high bar on financial inclusion and restrict outbound flows of money unless they are used for trading or transferred to depositary banking institutions. Banks have established privileged agreements with MTOs, who levy significant taxes on transfers. This serves as an additional tax on the poor and on the remittance system, which is an economic mainstay (Watkins and Quattri, 2014). Efforts to widen financial inclusion, possibly through the use of mobile money or alternative banking systems, would allow savings and transactions at the level of the individual, family or community to offer development benefits; it would reduce dependency on *hawala* systems, which may also be used as infrastructure for the criminal economy; and it would allow money to be protected from rent-seeking protection payments by all manner of actors. Experiences in East Africa have also shown that moving towards phone banking for payment of government services has reduced low-level bribe-paying and corruption, while increasing government revenue (World Bank, 2014).

A second implication of the dominance of the informal financial system and illicit trade is that West Africa's share of global flows is undervalued, affecting the standing of its balance of payments and global trade. This is a problem stemming not only from trade mispricing or invoicing – although this remains a significant IFF loss – but also arises from informal production activities going unrecorded. The AGSM case study highlights the sheer size of the informal sector, and the amount lost by gold-producing countries through diversionary activities and cross-border smuggling (OECD, forthcoming a). Realising the value of these potential revenues and resources through legitimate economic performance would enhance the region's capacity to engage in global and regional trade, and would allow economies to grow, reduce their aid dependency and generate long-term economic and social benefits.

Responses based solely on security strategies are not effective

If national governments and the development community wish to make meaningful progress on addressing IFFs, a combination of carefully tailored multisectoral policy instruments and approaches is needed to complement existing sanction and interdiction efforts. National governments and the international community have tended to rely heavily on law enforcement, border control and legal strategies as the predominant response to criminal economies. Yet the law enforcement officials interview for this study, both from the region and internationally, underlined a range of concerns undermining their effectiveness, including: areas of instability with little state authority or presence; communities and cities where smuggling is a livelihood strategy and economic dependency on those activities is high; long and porous borders that make credible border enforcement impossible; and weak institutions with limited capacity, resources or political support for sustained investigations. This report has identified some of the essential underpinnings of more effective responses – i.e. promoting sustainable livelihoods, financial inclusion and strategies to ensure integrity in the public service – which can complement and enhance the effectiveness of security and law-enforcement measures. Overall, however, considerably more research and learning is needed to identify the development conditions engendering or exacerbating IFFs, and their resulting impacts on a country's growth, security and development.

While devising a new law might make the practice illegal, it will not change behaviour unless other incentives are adopted. Many of the activities described in this report are, in fact, informal livelihood strategies, and little is to be gained by criminalising those involved.

Consistent and coherent regional strategies and responses are essential

A major finding of this study reinforces the need for Economic Community of West African States (ECOWAS) member countries to work together to develop and implement common or complementary strategies and policies across an inter-disciplinary set of policy areas, such as trade and investment, taxation and subsidy regimes, finance and banking, labour market regulation and migration. Given the significant degree of interdependence among countries in the region, it is clear that unilateral action on the part of one country will only have limited impact. Such action is more likely to displace rather than reduce criminal economies and IFFs. Across the board of criminal economies, smugglers and traffickers exploit differentials in tax regimes, or differences in surveillance capacities, to maximise their profits and minimise interdiction risks; this is particularly true in illicit trade in legal goods and illicit resource extraction, where the commodities or acts play an important role in the local economy. Even with purely illegal activities like drug trafficking, perpetrators exploit arbitrage opportunities between justice systems to practice their trade in areas with the least chance of detection and prosecution, and ensure the lowest levels of penalties if caught. Given the differences across countries, a regional strategy is a necessary, albeit insufficient, component of an effective response.

The ECOWAS region is not short on strategies, initiatives or declarations at the regional level. The necessary legislation is often in place to provide a framework for response, although implementation is often weak. Given the number of criminal economies in the region, and the relatively low capacity and resources available to address them, national and international policy makers seeking to address these challenges will need to choose their battles. Setting priorities – the entry point – will necessarily involve a careful balancing of trade-offs or factors. A few quick wins – "low-hanging fruit" – can be seized, but in the vast majority of cases, achieving results will require a long-term partnership between countries in the region and international actors. Once priorities are selected, maintaining a sustained focus and not spreading resources too thinly – or allowing them to be diverted to new issues – will be key.

It should be noted that West Africa is only one part of a global supply chain for the activities reviewed in this study and cannot alone be expected to address these criminal economies. The co-operation of OECD member countries is essential in this matter, and concerted efforts will be needed to reduce the demand for these criminal economies within established economies. OECD member countries can play a far more rigorous and active role in addressing criminal economies and IFFs outside of the region, ensuring that adequate attention is given to both the supply and demand sides of these criminal economies within the relevant economies. Priority should be given to shutting down the kinds of criminality that generate the most harm. In the case of illicit fishing or logging, for example, the European Union is the dominant consumer driving demand. Efforts to raise awareness and change consumer behaviour are one means to curb such illicit activities, but others can be explored. Subsidies and other related policies can also offset those industries where a large portion of trade is thought to have been illicitly sourced.

Common development principles should guide IFF responses

Dealing with criminal economies requires respecting the general principles that hold true for all cases and approaches:

Understand the political economy

Regulating the use and management of resources (whether licit or illicit) should be carefully handled, given the implications for the economy and society as a whole. A proper analysis of the political economy mapping the networks of interest behind the region's resources should be a prerequisite to any kind of intervention. In a similar vein, when seeking to intervene in criminal markets, it is important to consider that all flows – including development assistance – can have an impact on incentives and vested interests. In the past, development assistance has had a distortive effect on the economies of developing countries, particularly those with a high degree of informality.[3] The underlying principle must be to do no harm, which is not always assured when dealing with such complex issues.

Take a development perspective and avoid doing harm

The 2030 Agenda for Sustainable Development (2030 Agenda) signals that national governments and international donors share responsibility for achieving development, and that development objectives (i.e. growth, security, equity and inclusion – including financial inclusion) are best enabled by effective and accountable institutions (Sustainable Development Goal [SDG] 16). An IFF response strategy that applies heavy-handed, punitive measures to marginalised groups – for example, those whose livelihoods depend on subsistence activities – is likely to be counterproductive and will only increase criminal groups' social collateral within their host populations. It is particularly important for international efforts to ensure that all actions and rhetoric strive to "do no harm" in the context of these complex and contingent realities.

Various forms of criminal economies will always exist, even in the strongest states, but their impacts will be most detrimental when they use or result in violence. In these cases, the need to take action will likely outweigh any mitigating factors. In other cases, criminal trades may be firmly rooted in the local political economy with criminal groups offering benefits the state is unable to provide, such as income and employment, basic social services and security. In so doing, these groups can create alternative governance systems that compete with the state, particularly among populations lacking access to state services and protection – such as minority ethnic groups, immigrants in urban hubs or distant hinterland communities (Felbab-Brown, 2013; Reitano and Hunter, 2016). In such instances, an appropriate response may not be to attempt to tackle or deconstruct the prevailing illicit trade or economy; but rather, to enable slow, iterative and progressive change – including, for example, through the integration of such trades into the formal economy, and the development of strategies to rebuild the legitimacy of the state in relation to the host community.

Build reform coalition, involving state and non-state actors

Civil society groups and the media play a crucial role in developing and sharing knowledge about criminal economies, and catalysing action. They should be encouraged by the international community and national governments to play a greater role, particularly in demanding accountable governance. At the same time, the most informed and effective response efforts will be those that leverage the potential of multiple actors, including public officials, who have decision-making authority and some access to resources; the private sector, which may be affected and or in some way implicated in a given illicit activity; and non-state actors, including local leaders, civil society and community-based groups who can, for example, conduct research to drive reforms by national governments, or monitor implementation and action. Building effective coalitions for action will be essential to tackling the complex, multidimensional nature of the activity in question, as well as securing and deploying the diversity of skills that different actors can bring to the issue.

One of the major conclusions of this report is that drawing a line between informal and illegal activity in West Africa is a challenge; a number of practices that are considered illicit are, in fact, informal livelihood strategies. In these cases, there is little benefit from criminalising those involved in subsistence-level activities; other ways of modifying behaviour would result in a better outcome for society as a whole. By contrast, while elite diversion of resources may be legal – because the government defines the laws – the outcome is inherently wrong from the perspective of governance, justice and rule of law.

Social pressure can reinforce the use of laws and judicial tools, as well as market incentives and disincentives, to change norms and behaviours. Exposure, awareness raising and activism can promote or discourage behaviour at both the international and local levels, and signal that "business as usual" cannot continue. While the value of these activities in changing policies and standards should not be underestimated, no effort, no matter how well-intentioned or well-resourced, is likely to succeed without significant national leadership and ownership by the most implicated and affected stakeholders. The leadership, transparency and development focus of national governments will be critical to changing attitudes and diminishing the foundations that allow criminal economies to flourish at the regional, national or community level. Reducing or removing a criminal economy is a long-term effort that may take decades; the priorities are many, while the resources and capacity are thin.

Policy areas for further work

Organised crime has no boundaries: its effects are felt, variously, across fragile, developing, middle-income and developed countries. Poverty and inequality are clearly also linked to increases in illicit and criminal activity, e.g. human smuggling and trafficking, smuggling of counterfeit goods, environmental degradation, and extortion and bribery.

For too long, the security sector and criminal justice approaches have driven the responses to criminal economies, treating them solely as a law-enforcement issue. The Agenda 2030 clearly spells out the responsibility of development actors to address organised crime and the IFFs it produces. SDG 6.4 requires national governments and international actors to work together to "significantly reduce illicit financial and arms flows, strengthen recovery and return of stolen assets, and combat all forms of organised crime" by 2030. In addition to this direct mandate, organised crime and criminal economies cut across a range of development concerns; more than 20% of the Agenda 2030 targets are at risk from the harms of criminal economies (Global Initiative, 2014).

Thus, the responsibility of development actors is twofold: to directly address criminal economies and the systemic socio-economic and governance conditions that enable them; and to mitigate the impact of criminal economies on development objectives. There are no generic or linear sets of policy recommendations that can achieve this. Deliberate, problem-oriented policy formulation, negotiation and validation will be needed to develop multilevel (global, regional and national) responses that are relevant and tailored to the context. On a broad and provisional basis, this report recommends considering and further developing the following policy approaches as areas for first-order responses.

Financial and trade interventions

Trade regimes – i.e. the financial and regulatory environment at the international, regional and national levels – can either help or hinder the growth of criminal economies and the dispersal of IFFs outside of a country's productive formal economy. Given these challenges, this report recommends the following broad policy areas as areas in which IFFs mitigation measures could be designed and crafted:

Promote interregional trade and subsidy policies. Subsidies have an impact on the economic drivers related to illicit trade, and can serve as both incentives and deterrents. A free-trade zone is a step forward in this regard; however, as with other issues, the efficacy of this policy in countering illicit trade will depend on the level of implementation by national governments. The economies of West Africa are externally driven both on imports and exports, and there is minimal trade between countries of the region. Several empirical studies have shown the benefits of promoting interregional trade. For example, a 2005 study showed that trade within the West Africa Economic and Monetary Union could increase threefold if all intrastate roads were paved (UNCTAD, 2013). Promoting interregional trade would benefit local economies, and reduce their vulnerability to counterfeit goods and competing criminal economies. It may also reduce the propensity of the region's youth to look externally (to Europe or elsewhere) for employment opportunities and create a more region-centric economic environment. Regulatory and financial reform, including reducing the requirements for owning and operating a business, could promote business development by domestic actors.

Address problems of financial inclusion. Access to the formal banking system is out of reach for the majority of ordinary people in West Africa, and the principal means for remittance exchange and international transactions, the MTOs, are prohibitively expensive. Individual countries in the region could open the MTO industry to market competition, reducing privileged-partner agreements. They could also exploit the benefits of emerging technologies (e.g. mobile phone-based banking systems), which would promote higher degrees of financial inclusion. A further step would be to reduce petty and transactional corruption by encouraging electronic or mobile direct-pay systems for public services.

Take a nuanced approach to financial regulation. Given the dominance of the informal economy, and the extensive importance of *hawala* dealers for remittance transfers, efforts to enhance the capacity to combat terrorist financing and money laundering should be measured against the need to ensure that remittance flows can continue (Hammond, 2011). Both domestic and international financial regulators should aim for a more granular and vigilant approach to transfers by politically exposed persons (PEPs).

Strengthen IFF responses within OECD member countries. The OECD publication on IFFs, *Illicit Financial Flows from Developing Countries: Measuring OECD Responses* (OECD, 2014a), compared the performance of OECD member countries along a range of relevant international indicators. It found that OECD member countries are making significant progress in building the firewalls to counter IFFs. But work remains to be done, particularly to increase transparency of the financial system and corporate ownership, and monitor PEPs (OECD, 2014a). As a first step, all OECD member countries could comply with regulations, for example, by enhancing the capacity to identify and seize the assets of those PEPs known to be associated with criminal behaviours, and returning them to the source country. Given the clientelist nature of governance in West Africa, asset freezing and seizure – which could serve to reduce the capacity of powerbrokers to display their wealth – would send an important signal down the hierarchy of patronage networks.

Sharpen efforts to address the IFF risks arising at each step of the commodity supply chain. West African countries rely strongly on revenues from the extractive sector. The proceeds from Nigeria's oil and gas industry comprised 8.42% of its real gross domestic product (GDP)[4] and generated 75-80% of the country's overall government revenues in 2016. In Ghana extractive industries contributed to 10% of the GDP and 18% of the government revenues. Yet this sector is highly exposed to risks related to IFFs, as discretionary power and the politicisation of decision-making processes are major risks at various stages of the commodity's value chain. A 2014 OECD report showed that roughly one in five cases of transnational corruption took place in the extractive sector, ahead of arms dealing or public-infrastructure works which also have a more negative reputation (OECD, 2014b). Companies sourcing mineral resources are also strongly encouraged to carry out risk assessments across their whole supply chains. The OECD has developed a Due Diligence Guidance for Responsible Supply Chains of Minerals from Conflict-Affected and High Risk Areas (OECD, 2016), which provides detailed recommendations to help companies identify and address risks of contributing to conflict, adverse human-rights impacts and risks of corruption, bribery and money laundering, including through their mineral purchasing practices.

Align regulatory regimes behind efforts to counter illicit trade. The legal framework for world trade facilitates trade, but does not prevent illicit trading activity and in some cases WTO members seeking to regulate or control their borders can be challenged by other members before a WTO panel, which renders more challenging for countries to tackle IFFs. Global trade policies, such as the use of subsidies and tariffs, play an important role in defining and providing incentives for illicit trade. For example, within the WTO framework, a country exposed to high levels of inflows of counterfeit goods from other countries cannot claim damages or compensation from the originating or source countries. In the realm of intellectual property, there is no standardised offence categorised as counterfeiting which prevents extradition or legal action in another country. International free trade zones play an important role in global trade, and yet their proliferation has also increased vulnerabilities to illicit and criminal economies. Legislation regulating free trade zones is not standardised, and several countries do not apply national jurisdiction over goods in transit or goods in free trade zones (ICC, 2013). The infrastructure of legitimate trade, shipping lines, online sales sites, courier services and international payment solutions fulfil essential roles in enabling and facilitating trade; and yet, the liabilities of these international operators is limited when criminals abuse their services.

Incentivise good governance by corporations based in OECD member countries. Foreign corporations in West Africa, including those of OECD member countries, have been criticised for a range of practices. These include maximising profits through preferential tax regimes, failure to adhere to environmental and labour standards and outright criminal behaviour. To maintain their legitimacy, OECD member countries are encouraged to continue to address these issues within corporations headquartered in their own states building on previous achievements made under the Convention on Combating Bribery of Foreign Public Officials in International Business Transaction. These measures could be undertaken in parallel with efforts to strengthen the capacity of West African governments and private sector to fight corruption, including for example, through joint efforts such as the Joint African Development Bank-OECD Initiative to Support Business Integrity and Anti-Bribery Efforts in Africa.

Local livelihood and public-service provision

Recreate the link between governance and service provision. Criminal economies have enriched local interest groups at the expense of the state, enabling them to build legitimacy by offering security, livelihood and basic services to local communities, and any long-term goal of any intervention should be to reinforce the state's capabilities and legitimacy in the eyes of the public. Efforts will also need to resonate with communities, and should address their context driven priorities and vulnerabilities. Community priorities can be understood and addressed, perhaps using community-perception surveys, which can help to show which groups have gained social legitimacy. Participatory strategic planning and programme design, even around relatively small investments, can reinforce the likelihood that communities feel their needs have been met and priorities considered.

Building the legitimacy of the state is not straightforward. Criminal or terrorist groups may have achieved a degree of social legitimacy, and interventions that increase the insecurity of local populations will draw criticism and build resentment among them, particularly if there are no livelihood dividends attached. This threatens the buy-in and credibility of peace and state-building processes, and strengthens the legitimacy of the alternate governance provider – whether a criminal or terrorist group. In cases where the credibility of the state has been eroded over time or owing to widespread impunity, the state may not be able to move forward immediately. Alternative interlocutors, such as religious authorities and diaspora populations, could bridge the gap (Reitano and Hunter, 2016).

Support alternative livelihoods. One of the factors underpinning the prevalence of illicit trade in West Africa and individual involvement in criminal enterprises is the lack of viable livelihood alternatives. While job creation is a classic development strategy to reduce the appeal of illicit trafficking for former combatants, livelihood strategies often offer little more than short-term, labour-intensive work that cannot compare to the potent allure of illicit profits and genuinely sustainable livelihoods. To effectively address criminal economies, livelihood and employment-generation programmes will need to be done differently.

Studies of responses to organised crime in other contexts are useful. They have shown that to reach the target demographic, i.e. youth susceptible to criminal behaviour and violence, alternative livelihoods need to provide employment that enhances social standing and provides a viable future (Hoyos, Rogers and Székely, 2015). Other studies have observed that individuals attracted to illicit industries may have a higher risk tolerance, and that traditional employment generation and livelihood programmes might not appeal to them (Dercon, 2015). Innovation and experimentation are needed to find apprenticeship models and employment schemes that provide goals and achievement benchmarks, returns on perseverance and commitment, and investment opportunities that can generate sustainable livelihoods and social capital over the long term.

Justice and security

Traditionally, law enforcement, criminal justice and security-sector responses have been the dominant means of responding to criminal economies. This study has emphasised the limited efficacy of isolated responses, particularly in states where corruption and socio-economic drivers contribute to the enabling environment. Therefore, these recommendations cannot be expected to have an impact in isolation from other actions, but will continue to form part of a comprehensive and integrated solution.

Address the backward and forward linkages across the criminaljustice chain. To disrupt criminal and trafficking networks effectively, attention must be paid to ensuring appropriate levels of political will; legal frameworks that facilitate interdiction, leading to the arrest of higher-level traffickers; and capacity within the criminal-justice system to prosecute the individuals involved. Seizures and arrests will have a minimal impact if they are not followed up with appropriate levels of prosecution; however, judicial independence and integrity must also be assured. Penal reform and appropriate human-rights standards in prisons are important measures to prevent recidivism or the exacerbation of criminal environments. Areas rife with religious fundamentalism and terrorist ideologies should develop specialised capacity to deal with individuals susceptible to undergoing further radicalisation.

Pursue regional approaches. Given the transnational nature of criminal economies and criminal operations, the efficacy of any surveillance, sanction and interdiction efforts will have to extend beyond national borders. Moreover, unilateral law-enforcement strategies can experience the "balloon effect," where successful efforts in one country simply push the problem elsewhere. Co-ordinating efforts across countries and regions, including through sharing intelligence and joint operations, and aligning legal frameworks, can increase their effectiveness. Although addressing the issue from a regional perspective presents challenges; efforts to counter criminal economies should consider the regional implications and seek ways to align efforts across the region and with neighbouring regions. International donors and other multilateral actors can support co-ordination and information sharing.

Harmonise legal policy. Criminal networks have shown skill at hopping jurisdictions to select the most favourable conditions. ECOWAS member states will need to work together to counter criminal economies, ensuring consistent follow-through and reinforcing policy linkages between criminal justice, trade and development.

Innovate and adapt strategies to tackle corruption. Criminal economies and IFFs benefit from varying forms of corruption (by local police, border guards and local authorities) through impunity at the highest levels of the state and judiciary. If national and regional leaders do not take initiative on the issue of corruption, other strategic opportunities (such as internationally supported elections or transitions) can build mechanisms and bulwarks against corruption into certain contexts.

At the national level, some African countries have tried to reduce petty corruption through e-payments and mobile banking (Joseph, 2015). If ubiquitously applied to government services and key areas susceptible to corruption, this approach could reduce the size of the informal economy, and the widespread perception of corruption and impunity in governance (Zimmerman, Bohling and Rotman Parker, 2014). Although independent corruption commissions have a poor track record in sub-Saharan Africa, they have been effective elsewhere,[5] and could address elite corruption and impunity.

Update approaches of financial intelligence units (FIUs) to address informality: a relatively comprehensive set of existing programmes reinforce the capacity of FIUs to respond to money laundering and IFFs, yet a large number of transactions enabling the criminal economy are occurring in the informal sector through unregulated money transfer systems, such as *hawala.* Different countries have experimented with regulating and licensing *hawala* dealers, dedicating capacity within FIUs to overseeing remittance-service providers (Financial Action Task Force, 2013). Further research and new approaches to better address these linkages could be further explored. FIUs could also work to enhance their capacity to detect and respond to money laundering in the real-estate sector and other relevant sectors where funds have been invested.

Specialised independent organised crime units. The creation of specialised units to combat organised crime has been controversial; as in other jurisdictions, organised crime groups have targeted these units for corruption. Further, the isolation in which these units operate does not always translate into better co-ordination or capacity development of the broader police service (Center for International Policy, 2014). If designed with appropriate levels of independence and insulated against political influence, these units could be an effective means of investigating and prosecuting organised criminal groups and networks. In some countries, international sting operations have proven valuable in disrupting criminal networks at a high level; this capacity should be developed and led within the countries and regions (Reitano and Shaw, 2013).

Focus on service delivery and community-level policing. Strengthening relations between the police and the community, and enhancing public perceptions of – and trust in – policing is an important long-term intervention that would counteract longstanding corruption and redress the dominance of military actors over civilian policing units. Paying adequate police salaries is a prerequisite, as is including service-delivery metrics in assessments of police performance. Creating discretionary local funds that can be allocated to community-safety priorities can be valuable in building the confidence of local populations. Creation of ombudsman offices and other means of discreet provision of intelligence and information can help build a culture of reporting on illicit activity.

Notes

1. Several studies have shown, for example, that profits derived from trafficking cocaine are no more stigmatised than those from smuggling semolina (Meagher, 2005; Scheele, 2012; OECD/SWAC, 2014; Reitano and Shaw, 2015). This makes it still more difficult to disentangle the illegal from the informal and draw a line at where livelihoods end and criminality begins.
2. Per FATF (2013), the term *hawala* refers to a money transfer mechanism operating as a closed system within corridors linked by family, tribe or ethnicity. Used extensively along traditional trade routes in Asia, Middle East and East Africa centuries ago, in recent times the term has been used to describe a typology of money transmitters which arrange for transfer and receipt of funds or equivalent value and settle through trade, cash, and net settlement over a long period of time. *Hawala* and other similar service provider include hundi and underground banking.
3. Cases in Burundi (Brachet and Wolpe, 2005) and Somalia (Harvard, 2012), as well as in other countries, have shown that the delivery of humanitarian and development assistance can be co-opted by different actors and become another tool granting power and control to non-state armed groups.
4. In 2014, Nigeria's GDP was rebased from about USD 270 billion to USD 510 billion for 2013. The increase of 89% was attributed to new sectors of the economy such as

telecommunications, movies, and retail which were previously not captured or underreported.

5. One model of an internationally supported corruption court is the International Commission against Impunity in Guatemala. While not without flaws, it has proven effective at creating a bulwark between political and state office, corruption and aggressive infiltration by organised crime. For a comprehensive evaluation of the court, see WOLA (2015). Indonesia's KPK is another anti-corruption commission that has achieved positive results (Bolongaita, 2010).

References

Bolongaita, E. (2010), "An exception to the rule? Why Indonesia's anti-corruption commission succeeds where others don't – a comparison with the Philippines' ombudsman", *U4 Issue*, Vol. 2010(4), Chr Michelsen Institute, Bergen, www.u4.no/publications/an-exception-to-the-rule-why-indonesia-s-anti-corruption-commission-succeeds-where-others-don-t-a-comparison-with-the-philippines-ombudsman.

Brachet, J. and H. Wolpe (2005), "Conflict-sensitive development assistance: The case of Burundi", *Social Development Papers: Conflict Prevention and Reconstruction*, Paper No. 27, June 2005, World Bank, Washington, DC.

Burgis, T. (2015), *The Looting Machine: Warlords, Smugglers, Oligarchs and the Theft of Africa's Wealth*, Public Affairs, New York.

Center for International Policy (2014), "US security assistance to Honduras", *Security Assistance Monitor*, December 2014, Center for International Policy, Washington, DC, www.securityassistance.org/sites/default/files/USE_Honduras_English1.pdf.

Chayes, S. (2015), *Thieves of State: Why Corruption Threatens Global Security*, Norton and Company, London and New York.

Dercon, S. (2015), *Rightful Refugees, Managed Migrants: Development and Migration Crises*, Department for International Development, London.

ECA (2013), *The State of Governance in Africa: The Dimension of Illicit Financial Flows as a Development Challenge,* United Nations Economic Commission for Africa, Addis Ababa, www1.uneca.org/Portals/cgpp/2013/CGPP-3_Illicit-Financial-Flow-English_Final.pdf.

ECA (2012), *Report on the Magnitude of and Tools for Measuring Informal Cross-Border Trade in Africa's Regional Economic Communities,* Eighth Session of the Committee on Trade, Regional Co-operation and Integration, United Nations Economic Commission for Africa, Addis Ababa.

Felbab-Brown, V. (2013), "The purpose of law enforcement is to make good criminals? How to effectively respond to the crime-terrorism nexus", presentation to Convergence of Crime and Terrorism?, Arlington, 21 November 2013, www.brookings.edu/research/presentations/2013/11/21-how-effectively-respond-crime- terrorism-nexus-felbabbrown.

Global Initiative (2014), *Organized Crime as Cross-Cutting Threat to Sustainable Development: Measuring and Monitoring Transnational Organized Crime within the Framework of Sustainable Development for the Post-2015 Development Agenda*, Global Initiative against Transnational Organized Crime, Geneva.

Hammond, L. et al. (2011), *Cash and Compassion: The Role of the Somali Diaspora in Relief, Development and Peacebuilding*, United Nations Development Programme Somalia, Nairobi.

Harvard (2012), *Countering Terror in Humanitarian Crises: The Challenges of Delivering Aid to Somalia*, Programme on Humanitarian Policy and Conflict Research, Harvard University, Boston.

Hoyos, R., H. Rogers and M. Székely (2015), *Out of School and Out of Work: Risk and Opportunities for Latin America's Ninis*, World Bank, Washington, DC.

ICC (2013), *Free Trade Zones*, International Chamber of Commerce, Geneva.

Joseph, O. (2015), "Electronic payment system in Nigeria: Its economic benefits and challenges", *Journal of Education and Practice*, Vol. 6/16, International Knowledge Sharing Platform, http://iiste.org/Journals/index.php/JEP/article/view/23320.

Meagher, K. (2005), "Social capital or analytical liability?" Social networks and African informal economies", *Global Networks*, Vol. 5/3, Blackwell Publishing Ltd & Global Networks Partnership, Oxford, pp. 217-238.

OECD (forthcoming a), "Case study: The artisanal and small-scale gold mining sector", OECD Publishing, Paris.

OECD (forthcoming b), "Case study: Illicit narcotics transiting West Africa", OECD Publishing, Paris.

OECD (2016), *OECD Due Diligence Guidance for Responsible Supply Chains of Minerals from Conflict-Affected and High-Risk Areas: Third Edition*, OECD Publishing, Paris, http://dx.doi.org/10.1787/9789264252479-en.

OECD (2014a), *Illicit Financial Flows from Developing Countries: Measuring OECD Responses*, OECD Publishing, Paris. http://dx.doi.org/10.1787/9789264203501-en.

OECD (2014b), *OECD Foreign Bribery Report: An Analysis of the Crime of Bribery of Foreign Public Officials*, OECD Publishing, Paris. http://dx.doi.org/10.1787/9789264 226616-en.

OECD (2014), *An Atlas of the Sahara-Sahel: Geography, Economics and Security*, OECD Publishing, Paris, http://dx.doi.org/10.1787/9789264222359-en.

Reitano, T. and M. Hunter (2016), *Contests and Compacts: Organised Crime and Service Delivery*, International IDEA, Stockholm.

Reitano, T. and M. Shaw (2015), *Fixing a Fractured State? Breaking the Cycles of Crime, Corruption and Conflict in Mali and the Sahel*, Global Initiative against Transnational Organized Crime, Geneva.

Reitano, T. and M. Shaw (2013) *The End of Impunity? After the Kingpins, What Next for Guinea-Bissau?*, Institute for Security Studies, Pretoria.

Shaw, M. (2016), "'We pay, you pay': Protection economies, financial flows and violence", in *Beyond Convergence*, National Defense University, Washington, DC.

UNCTAD (2013), *Economic Development in Africa, 2013: Inter-African Trade, Unlocking Private Sector Dynamism*, United Nations Conference on Trade and Development, Geneva.

Watkins, K. and M. Quattri (2014), *Lost in Intermediation: How Excessive Charges Undermine the Benefits of Remittances for Africa*, Overseas Development Institute, London.

WOLA (2015), *The International Commission against Impunity in Guatemala (CICIG), A WOLA Report on the CICIG Experience*, Washington Office on Latin America, Washington, DC.

World Bank (2014), *Global Financial Development Report 2014: Financial Inclusion*, World Bank, Washington, DC.

Zimmerman, J.M., K. Bohling and S. Rotman Parker (2014), *Electronic G2P Payments: Evidence from Four Lower-Income Countries*, Consultative Group to Assist the Poor, World Bank, Washington, DC.

Interviews

SEN-GIABA-130515, Multiple senior research and policy officers, GIABA, in person, 13 May 2015. NE-Gov-LE-220915, Chief of Investigations, National Police, Niger, in person, 22 September 2015. WA-EUSec-120515, Multiple European Security Liaisons in West Africa, in person, 12 May 2015. WA-EU-080515, EU/UN project leader on AML in West Africa, by Skype, 8 May 2015.

UK-Gov-LE-220615, UK law enforcement officials working on IFFs and Africa, in person, 22 June 2015. USA-Gov-LE-120515, USA DEA Official in a West African country, in person, 12 May 2015.

Further reading

Alemika, E. (2013), *The Impact of Organised Crime on Governance in West Africa*, Friedrich-Ebert-Stiftung, Abuja.

Borgers, M. and H. Moors (2007), "Targeting the proceeds of crime: Bottlenecks in international cooperation", *European Journal of Crime, Criminal Law and Criminal Justice*, Vol. 15/2, pp. 1- 22.

Cockayne, J. (2014), *Strengthening Mediation to Deal with Criminal Agendas*, Centre for Humanitarian Dialogue, Geneva.

CPJ (2015), *Journalists killed since 1992* (database), Committee to Protect Journalists, www.cpj.org/killed (accessed 20 March 2015).

FATF (2013), *The Role of Hawala and Other Similar Service Providers in Money Laundering and Terrorist Financing*, Financial Action Task Force, Paris.

Lacher, W. (2013), "Challenging the myth of the drug-terror Nexus in the Sahel", *Background Paper*, No. 4, West Africa Commission on Drugs, Geneva.

Powell, J. (2014), *Talking to Terrorists: How to End Armed Conflicts*, Random House, London.

Reporters Without Borders (21 November 2013), "Côte d'Ivoire a threatening environment for journalists", Reporters Without Borders, http://en.rsf.org/cote-d-ivoire-threatening-environment-for-21-11-2013,45490.html.

Scheele, J. (2012), *Smugglers and Saints of the Sahara*, Cambridge University Press, Cambridge.

Annex A.
Research methodology

Methodology

The following methodology applies to the scoping or baseline study, the more detailed case studies (to be published as Working Papers) and this final synthesis report.

Desk research: the main body of this report is derived from a comprehensive review of the secondary literature from a wide range of sources, including national reports, studies and strategies, international and civil- society reports, the academic literature and the news media. More than 1 000 individual documents and sources in three languages (English, French and Portuguese) were consulted. In addition, approximately 200 primary data sets were reviewed, mined and analysed for trends relating to the continent as a whole and to the subregion specifically. More than 200 individual sources are quoted directly in the report.

This methodological approach, and consequently the study's findings, is heavily influenced by the literature available on the subject. The quality of the available secondary literature varies according to the geographic and subject-matter focus. As such, the study is as much a review of the discussion surrounding criminal economies and illicit financial flows (IFFs) in West Africa as it is an assessment of the scale and impact of illicit activity. A further challenge is the absence or weakness of data available in the region. Nevertheless, the report can claim that data and statistics are taken from internationally recognised actors and sources, and that it is an accurate portrayal of the secondary literature and analysis available on the subject.

One lead author, Tuesday Reitano, co-ordinated the preparation and drafting of the report, and co-edited the case studies with the OECD. A team of five experts from the Global Initiative against Transnational Organized Crime[1] also contributed: Karl Lallerstedt, Rob McCusker, Mark Shaw, Marcena Hunter and Theodore Coutts of the World Bank, as well as a number of research assistants: Iris Oustinoff, Adam Rodriques, Mohammed Sesay and Jessica Gerken. The authors and contributors also called upon the expertise and experience of the more than 250 members of the Global Initiative Network of Experts, as well as on subject-matter experts in different OECD directorates. Combining this expertise with the authors' own knowledge, the study brings to bear a diverse range of thematic and regional experiences, and the relevant technical skills. In particular, the study benefits from decades of research and partnership by the authors with national institutions and civil-society organisations in West Africa itself, as well as their fieldwork in various countries in the region over several years prior to this study. This allows for a comprehensive and current assessment of trends and phenomena.

Key informant interviews: 100 key informants were interviewed for this study, covering a wide range of interlocutors and global experts. These included policy makers, practitioners, law-enforcement officials and analysts in the OECD, the United Nations and other multilateral bodies, as well as independent non-governmental organisations and think tanks, both internationally and in the region itself. Interviews were also conducted with both national and international journalists who have investigated and reported on West Africa.

Field research: the report, and in particular the understanding of the implications of criminal economies and IFFs, benefitted from five in-depth case studies by experts in their respective fields. Each case study included a series of field visits to between one and three countries, as well as to OECD member countries. Interviews were conducted with national and international representatives of state institutions, the private sector, civil society and affected communities. They were also conducted with international policy makers, practitioners and independent experts from elsewhere in the world, including OECD member countries, as required to ensure comprehensive information and perspectives. Table A.1 summarises the interviews undertaken over the course of the study.

Table A.1.**Interviews conducted for the study**

Interview code	Interview description
NE-Gov-LE-220915	Chief of investigations, National Police, Niger, 22 September 2015
WA-IOM-130515	Immigration and border management specialist, IOM, in Dakar, 13 May 2015
SEN-GIABA-130515	Multiple senior research and policy officers, GIABA, 13 May 2015
UK-Gov-LE-220615	Multiple national crime agency officers, United Kingdom, 22 June 2015
CAD-Analyst-220615	Professor of law and population, international university, 22 June 2015
VIE-UNODC-030515	Africa crime expert, international organisation, 3 June 2015
NIG-Corp-Auto-120615	Automotive industry engineer, multinational corporation (international), 14 June 2015
GHA-Corp-Agri-1000615	Corporate affairs manager, company providing product integrity solutions (Ghana), 10 June 2015
GHA-Gov-090615	Chief executive, government authority in Ghana, 9 June 2015
GHA-Gov-LE-110615	Chief executive, government law-enforcement entity (Ghana), 11 June 2015
GHA-Gov-110615	Chief executive and Head of research, government agency (Ghana), 11 June 2015
GHA-Corp-Pharma-120615	Deputy director, government agency (Ghana), 12 June 2015
GHA-IO-Econ-180615	Economist, international organisation (Ghana), 18 June 2015
GHA-Corp-Finance-200915	Secretary-General, business association in Ghana, 20 September 2015
GHA-Corp-Agri-120615	Programme manager, business association in Ghana, 12 June 2015
GHA-Gov-Drug-090615	Government official (drugs), government authority in Ghana, 9 June 2015
USA-Gov-Hum-190515	International Aid Expert, government aid agency (international aid agency), 19 May 2015
GHA-Journ-120615	Investigative journalist, media organisation (Ghana), 12 June 2015
GHA-Gov-LE-120615	Law enforcement officer, law enforcement agency (Ghana), 12 June 2015
GHA-Gov-LE-290515&100615	Law enforcement officer, foreign embassy in Ghana, 29 May 2015 and 10 June 2015
GHA-Gov-Pharm-100615	Director, government ministry (Ghana), 10 June 2015
GHA-Gov-LE-100615	Head of special government entity (Ghana), 10 June 2015
GHA-INGO-Pharm-120615	Pharmaceutical expert, international NGO (Ghana), 12 June 2015
NGA-Analyst-250615	Senior analyst, consulting firm (Nigeria), 25 June 2015
GHA-Gov-Justice-100615	Senior Justice Representative, government of Ghana, 10 June 2015
GHA-Corp-Agri-090515	Technical advisor, industry association (Ghana office), 9 June 2015
NGA-Corp-Trade-030715	West Africa anti-illicit trade manager, multinational corporation (Nigeria), 3 July 2015
UK-Gov-Policy-220615	Senior strategy and co-ordination officer, UK Home Office, 22 June 2015
SEN-EUGov-Justice-120515	Senior liaison of a European embassy to Justice Ministry Senegal, 12 May 2015
UK-Gov-Analyst-230615	Africa research analysts, UK-FCO, 23 June 2015
WA-CivSoc-130515	Multiple research and policy officers, West Africa office security-focused pan-African NGO, 13 May 2015
WA-EUSec-120515	Multiple European security liaisons in West Africa, 12 May 2015
WA-UNODC-020615	UNODC senior research officer in West Africa, by Skype, 2 June 2015
WA-UNODC-290615	UNODC research officer in West Africa, by phone, 29 May 2015
WA-EU-080515	EU/UN project leader on AML in West Africa, by Skype, 8 May 2015

Table A.1. **Interviews conducted for the study** (*continued*)

Interview code	Interview description
GHA-Analyst-190615	Senior official, West Africa-based security-focused NGO policy and training centre, by Skype, 19 June 2015
VIE-UNODC-290515	Senior UNODC official, by Skype, 29 May 2015
UK-Gov-LE-220515	Senior liaison officer, UK-NCA, by phone, 22 May 2015
USA-Gov-LE-120515	USA DEA Official in a West African country, 12 May 2015
NIG-DrugTrafficker-100915	Nigerian drug trafficker in Johannesburg, 10 September 2015
POR-Gov-Diplo-280515	Multiple security and co-operation Affairs representatives from a European Embassy in West Africa, written response to questions, 28 May 2015
POR-Gov-Diplo-290515	Multiple security and co-operation affairs representatives from a European embassy in West Africa, by Skype, 29 May 2015
GHA-Analyst-160615	Academic researcher, by phone, 16 June 2015
GHA-Analyst-230615	Academic researcher, by phone, 23 June 2015
GHA-CivSoc-110515	Civil society actor, 11 May 2015
GHA-CivSoc-160515	Civil society actor, by phone, 16 June 2015
LBR-CivSoc-200515	Civil society actor, Liberia, 20 May 2015
LBR-CivSoc-210515	Civil society actor, Liberia, 21 May 2015
LBR-CivSoc-230515	Civil society actor, Liberia, 23 May 2015
GHA-Analyst-041115	Analyst, Ghana, by email, 4 November 2015
GHA-Finan-130515	Financial Intelligence Officer, Ghana, 13 May 2015
LBR-GERGov-180515	Foreign official, Liberia, 18 May 2015
LBR USGov 200515	Foreign official, Liberia, 20 May 2015
GHA-Gov-140515	Government administrator, Ghana, 14 May 2015
GHA-Analyst-110515	Independent expert, Ghana, 11 May 2015
NOR-Analyst-300415	Independent expert, 30 April 2015
GHA-IO-150515	International organisation representative, Ghana, 15 May 2015
LBR-IO-020615	International organisation representative, by phone, 2 June 2015
LBR-Journ-200515	Journalist, Liberia, 20 May 2015
LBR-IO-210515	Konah Karmo, Liberia, Extractive Industries Transparency Initiative, 21 May 2015
GHA-Corp-Min-120515	Mining consultant (buyers), Ghana, 12 May 2015
GHA-Gov-Min-150515	Official at Minerals Commission, Ghana, 15 May 2015
LBR-Corp-Min-180515	Mining industry representative, Liberia, 18 May 2015
LBR-Corp-Min-190515	Mining industry representative, Liberia, 19 May 2015
GHA-Gov-Min-130515	Senior mining advisor, Ghana, 13 May 2015
GHA-Gov-130515	State official, Ghana, 13 May 2015
LBR-Gov-210515	State official, Liberia, 21 May 2015
UK-Gov-Sec-230615	Financial flows analyst, JNAC, Ministry of Defense, 23 June 2015
RDV-SCLCT-22092015	Police captain, Chief of investigations, SCLCT, 22 September 2015
NIG-Gov-LE-201015	Multiple Nigerian officers of the Financial Intelligence Unit and National Risk Assessment Secretariat, Nigeria, 20 October 2015
NIG-Gov-Sec-121015	Joint Terrorism Analysis Branch: Office of the National Security Advisor, Nigeria, 19 October 2015

Note: Unless otherwise noted, the interviews were in person.

Quantitative research

Of the five case studies in this report, three – on human smuggling, counterfeits and terrorist financing – include original quantitative survey research (Table A.2). The interviews were conducted using an innovative person-to-person mobile phone-based research platform, Vibrand Reach.[2] This platform offers an extensive survey capacity working with local partners in local communities across Africa. It allowed a rapid survey of attitudes, perceptions and experiences within the time and budget limitations of the study.

The case study on human smuggling also included the findings of semi-structured interviews with migrants in migrant reception and processing centres, as well as at other locations in Italy.

Table A.2. **Overview of quantitative research**

	Countries conducted	Key questions	Number of respondents
Case study: Human smuggling			
Migrant source surveys	Nigeria, Ghana	– Do you know anyone who has migrated? – Where did they go? – Have they returned? Why? – How did they organise their trip? How much did they pay? – Would you migrate and why? – Where would you want to go? – How much would you be prepared to pay?	N = 429 Ghana = 229 Nigeria = 200 (All male)
Migrant destination surveys	Italy	The interviews were semi-structured around 6 key themes: – Motivation and decision to migrate – Experience of the migration journey – Experience with and payments to facilitators – Risks, difficulties and abuses experienced – Experiences with corruption or corrupt practices	N = 45
Case study: Counterfeits			
Consumer survey	Ghana	– Which types of counterfeit products have you experienced? – Has anyone tried to sell you fake goods? – Have you, or someone you know, purchased counterfeit goods? – How do you know whether what you are buying is real or fake? – Where do you think counterfeit goods come from? – How acceptable do you consider it to buy counterfeit products?	N = 314 Male = 177 Female = 136
Business survey	Ghana	Questions were semi-structured, conducted by telephone, with businesses selling the categories of goods in the study (agrochemicals, consumer goods, pharmaceuticals). Key themes explored: – What proportion of goods in your industry sold are fake? – What types of consumers buy fake products? – Where are fake products sold? – Have you been approached to sell fake products? – How would you know if the goods you sell are fake? – Have you ever been subject to government regulation? – How is the government dealing with the problem of fake goods?	N = 221 Agrochemicals = 70 Consumer goods = 70 Pharmaceuticals = 71

Source-country interviews on migration perceptions: a quantitative survey was commissioned in three West Africa countries: Gambia, Nigeria and Ghana. The surveys attempted to gauge attitudes towards migration in the source countries of the Economic Community of West African States (ECOWAS), as well as identify any change in attitudes or behaviour of migrant recruiters during the recent surge in migration. Gambia and Nigeria were selected because they account for the highest levels of arrivals in Europe of ECOWAS countries. Ghana was selected as a control in its capacity as another Anglophone country with a comparable socio- economic profile. Given the challenges in gaining permission from the local authorities, the Gambia survey could not be completed within the time available for this study. The survey had 429 respondents – 200 from Nigeria and 229 from Ghana – with two phases of surveying to allow verification of the methodology and results.

Destination-country migrant interviews: to ensure the case study reflected the most current situation and experiences, interviews with recently landed migrants were conducted at reception centres in southern Italy. Interviews were also held at migrant-processing centres in various cities across the country.

Of the interviews respondents, 45 were from ECOWAS, all were male, and 80% were between the ages of 18 and 25. Finding respondents who were female or older proved challenging. The countries represented in the study were Gambia (ten respondents); Nigeria (nine respondents); Mali (eight respondents); Côte d'Ivoire (seven respondents); Senegal (six respondents); and Ghana (three respondents); two individuals from other ECOWAS countries also responded. This is obviously a small sample, compared to the tens of thousands who have crossed to Europe in the recent migration crisis. However, it at least allowed a glimpse of the experiences faced by migrants.

The interviews were voluntary, taking the form of a semi-structured conversation. The five interviewers were provided with an indicative interview protocol, including over 50 questions divided among a range of themes. These included the motivations and original reason for migrating, the types and sources of information received before departure, the preferred destination, the route taken, the amount paid and the experiences along the way. The interviewers particularly probed for accounts of how the migrants were treated, and any experiences or concerns about abuse or extortion. Relevant demographic and socio-economic information was also collected.

Each semi-structured interview lasted approximately one hour. Participants were not expected to answer every question and were not pressed to discuss issues that made them feel uncomfortable. The responses were first reviewed in long form and then coded for statistical analysis.

Respondents were reluctant to discuss certain questions, particularly concerning the boat crossing. Despite their assurances, the interviewers had the impression respondents' reluctance may have been due to concerns on the purpose of the interview. All of the migrants interviewed were still waiting for their asylum claims to be processed and thus may have had fears of being returned.

Boko Haram financing: the case study on terrorist financing focused predominantly on the Sahel-based terrorist groups. It also benefited, however, from a parallel study on Boko Haram financing, which included a quantitative research component. Perception-based polls gauged public sentiment in northeast Nigeria on terrorism-related topics. Boko Haram is located in the region, and the general population is closely tied to the conflict, both as the target of attacks and as a main source of revenue for the group.

These surveys, along with all the other surveys conducted for this report, were conducted by Vibrand Research. They addressed not only the topic of Boko Haram, but also regional perceptions on safety, security, community activities, terrorist behaviours, the interactions between terrorists and local communities, and the efficacy of national and international counter-terrorism measures.

In total, two polls were administered: a 200-person exploratory poll split between two key cities and a subsequent 900-person poll split between three key cities. The exploratory poll was intended to survey 100 people in Maiduguri and 100 people in Mubi. However, due to a spike in terrorist attacks, as well as safety concerns for interviewers and interviewees, the polling was expanded to surrounding areas.

Based on the findings of the exploratory study, a larger polling campaign was initiated in Kano, Bauchi and Gombe, with a sample size of at least 300 individuals in each location and a 50-50 gender split. All locations were selected based on the level of Boko Haram presence and activity. The results were retrieved from Vibrand Research in September 2015.

The perception polls were carefully drafted to avoid biases and leading or loaded questions. The sample sizes were selected to retrieve statistically significant results. Since the results extracted from these polls are perception-based, they were integrated in a supplemental and corroborative capacity, as well as to set the context for discussions on Boko Haram.

Calculating the scale of internal and external illicit flows

This study has deliberately shied away from quantifying the scale and value of specific flows; For the reasons outlined earlier, it has emphasised understanding – rather than measuring – the impact of criminal economies and IFFs. However, for purposes of comparative analysis, Figure A.1 presents the best possible estimate of the total IFFs related to a series of criminal economies highlighted in the report, distinguishing between IFFs invested within and outside the region. Analyses of IFFs rarely make this distinction.

Any presentation of the value of illicit flows tends to be the subject of heated debate, largely because the flows are difficult to estimate and many measurement methodologies exist. Those presented in Figure A.1 are measured estimates, drawn from data provided by UN agencies, the World Bank and INTERPOL, or by recognised experts. This section aims to explain how the authors derived the numbers presented here, always using conservative estimates.

ASGM: it is difficult to assess the value of IFFs associated with ASGM and gold smuggling. One method compares production estimates with import and export figures. For example, in 2011, the United Arab Emirates imported 27.6 tonnes of gold from Ghana; however, Ghana reports exporting only 19.4 tonnes of gold to the United Arab Emirates in the same year (UN Comtrade, 2015). If all gold imported to the United Arab Emirates that reportedly came from Ghana did in fact originate there, this would mean that 30% was smuggled out of Ghana and only entered the formal supply chain upon import to the United Arab Emirates. Extrapolating from this figure, one could assume that 30% of gold is smuggled out of the country, valued at USD 720 million (US dollars) in 2013. Comparing production estimates in Liberia to the amount of gold officially exported shows that 86-90% of gold is smuggled out of the country (United Nations Security Council, 2013). In addition, an estimated 7 tonnes of gold was smuggled out of Burkina Faso in 2014 (Guéniat and White, 2015), valued at USD 256 million. When similar calculations are conducted using import and export figures for other gold-producing nations in West Africa, it is estimated that IFFs amount to over USD 3 billion. Due to the labour-intensive nature of the ASGM sector, a large portion (85%) of IFFs is believed to remain in the region, although individuals engaging in digging and mining are compensated very little per capita. It should be noted, however, that differences in export and import volumes do not necessarily reflect illicit financial flows. There may be other explanations for that. The calculation presented here aims to enable a discussion on the amounts of IFFs that remain in and leave the region.

Figure A.1. **Illustrative estimate of possible IFFs generated by criminal activity; proportion remaining in the region and leaving the region**

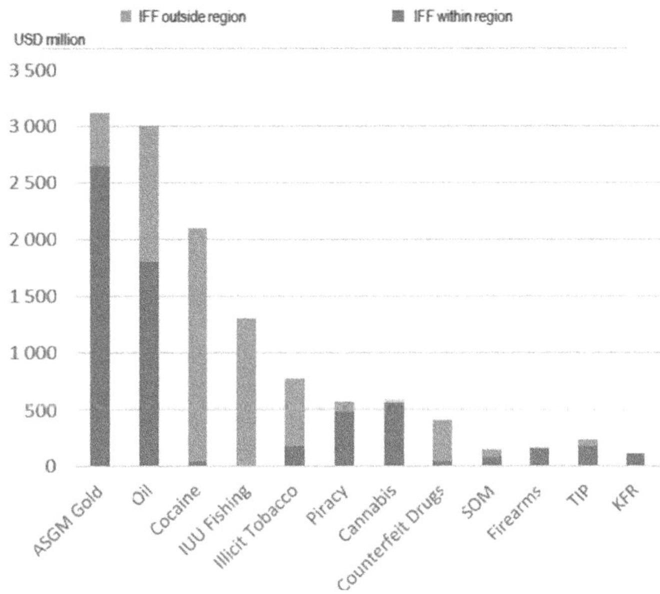

Notes: This estimate is produced for illustrative purposes and for the benefit of enabling a discussion on IFFs remaining in and leaving West Africa. Given the difficulties in ascertaining robust figures on this topic, the numbers in this graph should not be taken as definitive.

ASGM: artisanal and small-scale gold mining; IUU fishing: Illegal, unregulated and unreported fishing; SOM: smuggling of migrants; TIP: trafficking in persons); KFR: kidnap for ransom.

Source: Various, as explained below.

Oil theft: Chatham House published the most comprehensive account of oil theft in the Niger Delta in 2013 (Katsouris and Sayne, 2013). In this report, Nigeria was losing 100 000-250 000 barrels per day of its most valuable commodity, valued at approximately USD 3-8 billion per year, to fuel theft. A considerable portion of the oil moves across the border (see Chapter 3) for consumption in neighbouring countries, but this is considered an internal flow.

The report outlines the structure of fees and protection payments enabling the illicit trade, and notes that most beneficiaries are from the Nigerian elite. While the payments are used to maintain patronage networks, it is assumed a portion is also moved to overseas territories. Nigeria is considered to be the largest source of IFFs in Africa, with oil driving that total.

A 2003 investigation claimed that Nigeria could be losing as much as USD 600 million per year – approximately 40% of domestic production at that time – from the diversion of the stolen crude by international oil companies (Gboyega et al., 2011). The same 40%

proportion was therefore used to estimate the extent of diverted funds leaving the region, with the balance of the USD 3 billion estimated to remain in the region.

Cocaine: Chapter 3 examines the estimated total value of the cocaine flow through West Africa, and the percentage of that flow accrued in the region, based on a composite of the available best estimates from the sources consulted in the research.

An estimated 40 tonnes of cocaine per year moves through West Africa (UNODC, 2013). While it is valued at USD 2.1 billion per year, West African actors only earn an estimated USD 40 million per year for local "protection" or facilitation. Approximately three-quarters of that amount remains in the region to support local patronage networks or make local purchases, with the remainder invested externally. The 35-40 tonne estimate comes from the knowledge of Colombian traffickers active in the region, operating in smaller groups known as *cartelitos* (small cartels), who consider moving anything below 5 tonnes as unprofitable. Based on interviews by the United Nations Office on Drugs and Crime (UNODC) with inmates of West African prisons, about seven *cartelitos* operate in the region. The rough estimate of yearly tonnage comes from these conversations. Transactions for the purchase of large consignments are almost certainly made outside West Africa, with little if any of these funds flowing into the region.

IUU fishing: as outlined in Chapter 3, the fishing sector is a significant economic driver in the West African region, but a number of experts have estimated that the scale of illicit fishing as extensive. The Environmental Justice Foundation (EJF) has set global losses as a result of IUU fishing at USD 10-23.5 billion per year (accounting for between 11-26 million tonnes of fish) (EJF, 2012). In 2014, the Africa Progress Panel noted that "West Africa has some of the world's higher reported rates of IUU fishery activity, with one-third to one- half of the catch affected" and that West Africa could be suffering losses of up to USD 1.3 billion per year through IUU fishing (Africa Progress Panel, 2014). This report uses this figure, which is considered the most conservative and recent.

As studies of IUU fishing operations have shown, this illicit trade is perpetrated exclusively by international fishing vessels overfishing in the Gulf of Guinea and in the coastal waters of West African states; the produce is taken to markets in Europe and Asia. It is therefore assumed that – at best – negligible amounts of the value of this IFF remain in the region, perhaps earned through the illegal sale of fishing permits and corruption payments.

Illicit tobacco: in 2009, UNODC estimated that illicit cigarettes generate USD 774 million in annual revenue in the region (UNODC, 2009). The same study estimated, however, that 78% of this trade was transiting to Maghreb countries, where the illicit tobacco is consumed. While patterns have shifted following the post-revolutionary instability in Libya, this remains the best reliable and quantified available estimate of the trade.

Cannabis: the figures on illicit trade in cannabis are based on estimates in Ralston (2014), which multiplied the regional production (3 500 tonnes) by the average regional retail price (USD 0.17 per gramme). The retail price is the West African retail price, as the region virtually exports none of its cannabis abroad and grows it mainly for local consumption; thus, the region retains most of the value of the flow.

Counterfeit drugs: in 2013, the UNODC calculated conservatively that West Africa imported about USD 150 million worth of counterfeit medicine ever year (UNODC, 2013; Mackey and Liang, 2013). Other sources have produced far higher values – as high as USD 400 million per year for anti-malarial medication alone (Mackey and Liang,

2013). For this report, we opted for the higher range of the estimate, based on the findings of the counterfeit case study (Chapter 3) which suggested the value of fake medicines imported into Ghana alone could amount to USD 330 million, thereby making our high-end range still a conservative figure.

Most of the value of this flow accrues to the countries producing the counterfeit goods; a small portion – estimated by the authors at less than 10% of the total – goes toy regulators and border control through corruption, and to local vendors through sales.

Smuggling of migrants: the case study estimated that in 2015 3 000 migrants were departing from Agadez on a weekly basis (i.e. 156 000 per year) on convoys headed towards Libya, the primary gateway to Europe. The average cost of that portion of the voyage was USD 350. Based on migrant interviews and expert estimates, migrants are unlikely to have spent more than USD 100 on transportation and smugglers for their travel within the ECOWAS zone, prior to arriving in Agadez; the total cost of an individual migration journey within the ECOWAS zone was USD 450; the total value of migrant travel within ECOWAS, therefore, amounted to USD 148.2 million. However, in 2015, approximately 60 000 migrants of West African nationalities were registered in Europe (Frontex, 2014) including about one-half of migrants of "unspecified sub-Saharan" nationalities. The average cost of a sea passage at that time was USD 1 300. This meant that to reach Europe, West African nationals paid a further USD 78 million in total to actors outside the region to complete their migration journey, which would represent an additional IFF.

Piracy: estimates of the annual cost of piracy to West African countries range from USD 565 million to USD 2 billion, although the higher amount is driven by estimates of oil theft, either sourced from or transmitting through the Gulf of Guinea (Osinowo, 2015). To avoid double counting, the lowest estimate in the range was chosen for this report. The estimate of flows occurring internally were derived as 85% of the total; once oil theft is controlled for, the analysis suggests that robberies of cargo ships were perpetuated mainly by armed groups from the region (UNODC, 2013).

Human trafficking: the figures are based on the calculations in Ralston (2014), which in turn are taken from a 2009 study by UNODC. The total monetary value was estimated by multiplying the midpoint of UNODC estimates for the annual flow of humans trafficked for sexual exploitation out of West Africa (4 750) by the midpoint UNODC estimate of the price for one individual (USD 47 500). The estimates for the flow were originally obtained by assuming that an average of 1 out of 30 trafficked humans in Europe was detected.

The authors then drew their estimations based on the fact that most human-trafficking networks are Nigeria-based and perpetuated through diaspora connections, and that most of the flows (80% as a rough guide) would accrue within the region (Ellis, 2016).

This would not account for the enormous number of people in situations of human trafficking, or bonded, forced and child labour within the region (see Chapter 3). According to the definitions in this study, however, the flow would not be perceived as an IFF, but as an informal economy.

Firearms: the figures are based on Ralston (2014), which extrapolated the legal imports of ammunitions and firearms in West Africa, assuming that rebel and criminal groups at least match government purchases. As the flow of arms in the region is estimated to be almost entirely circular, with limited new stock (Anders, 2014), the value of these arms transactions remains almost entirely within the region.

Caveats

Criminal practices, both globally and in West Africa, are evolving quickly, and every effort was made to profile the current situation accurately. While the older literature was not discounted, the literature review prioritised current publications. All told, 75% of the literature cited was published in the last three years. In some cases, the phenomena – e.g. the smuggling of migrants to Europe, or the actions and financing of terrorist groups – are changing so rapidly that even recent reports now give a dated picture. In these cases, the news media, journalists and frontline practitioners became a dominant source; this may have limitations from an analytical point of view, and point-in-time analysis can skew longitudinal perspectives.

A number of challenges emerged when attempting to measure and analyse illicit activity in general, and IFFs in particular. Further, no metric is ever perfect. The measures presented in the past have been extensively debated, contested and criticised, particularly around several issues: over-reliance on trade mispricing as a proxy for all IFFs, and failures to account sufficiently for tax evasion (e.g. through jurisdiction hopping or tax havens) or illicit economic activity. Global studies have estimated that criminal activity represents about 35% of total IFFs (Boyce and Ndikumana, 2012). Other studies argue the share could be far greater in developing countries, where the informal economy is quite large. One study estimated the share of a national economy beyond state control could be as high as 90% for fragile states in sub-Saharan Africa (Grief, 1996). A later UNODC study confirmed this amount; it noted that the percentage of crime proceeds increased in developing countries, and that the funds generated were more likely to be laundered overseas (UNODC, 2011).

Measuring the quantity and value of the criminal economy also presented numerous challenges. Estimates are largely based on seizure data. While this can often be a useful indicator of changing trends, it has limitations; in the context of West Africa, these drawbacks are particularly prevalent. In the best-case scenario, seizures represent a maximum of 33% of the total flow in any context; arguably, they are often a better measure of law-enforcement capacity and integrity than of the scale of actual flows (UNODC, 2014). In the context of weak states and widespread corruption, the capacity of seizures to add value are significantly restricted; a reduction in the quantity of seizures may instead indicate greater state complicity and protection of those flows, rather than reduced IFFs (Midgley et al., 2014).

Reference groups and peer-review process

An expert Reference Group supported the report development and drafting process. It consisted of 22 representatives of OECD member states and multilateral institutions, recognised in the acknowledgement section. The Reference Group reviewed the inception report for the study in March 2015 to provide feedback on direction and priorities for the authors. Subject experts presented 13 forms of criminal economies reviewed in the inception report (and presented in this final report): 5 case studies were selected that were representative of the 3 typologies around which the report was structured, based upon a tiered voting system.

The peer-review process was structured around two stages. First, the OECD Development Co-operation Directorate reviewed draft case studies; between six and eight subject experts then reviewed the studies between June-August 2015. The studies were then finalised, incorporating the comments received. Second, the final full report was subjected to another peer-review process in early December 2015. Seventeen peer reviewers were involved, including members of the Reference Group, experts from dedicated divisions of the OECD, members of relevant civil-society organisations and recognised independent experts in the field of study. The peer reviewers who did not request anonymity are mentioned in the acknowledgement section.

Notes

1. www.globalinitiative.net.
2. www.vibrand.co.za.

References

Africa Progress Panel (2014), *Africa Progress Panel Report 2014: Grain, Fish, Money*, Africa Progress Panel, Geneva.

Anders, H. (2014), *Identifying Sources: Small-calibre Ammunition in Côte d'Ivoire*, Small Arms Survey, Geneva.

Boyce, J. and L. Ndikumana (2012), *Capital Flight from Sub-Saharan African Countries: Updated Estimates, 1970-2010*, Political Economy Research Institute, University of Massachusetts, Amherst.

EJF (2012), *Pirate Fishing Exposed: The Fight Against Illegal Fishing in West Africa and the EU*, Environmental Justice Foundation, London.

Ellis, S. (2016), *This Present Darkness: A History of Organized Crime in Nigeria*, Hurst Publishers, London.

Frontex (2014), *FRAN Quarterly*, July-September 2014 (Q3), Frontex, Warsaw.

Grief, A. (1996), "Contracting, enforcement and efficiency: Economics beyond the law", in Bruno, M. and B. Pleskovic (eds.), *World Bank Conference on Development Economics,* World Bank, Washington, DC.

Gboyega, A. et al. (2011), *Political Economy of the Petroleum Sector in Nigeria*, World Bank, Washington, DC.

Guéniat, M. and N. White (2015), *A Golden Racket: The True Source of Switzerland's "Togolese" Gold*, Berne Declaration, Geneva.

Katsouris, C. and A. Sayne (2013), *Nigeria's Criminal Crude: International Options to Combat the Export of Stolen Oil*, Chatham House, London.

Mackey, T.K. and B.A. Liang (2013), "Improving global health governance to combat counterfeit medicines: A proposal for a UNODC-WHO-Interpol trilateral mechanism", *BMC Medicine*, Vol. 11/233, University of California, San Diego.

Midgley, T. et al. (2014), *Defining and Measuring the Stress Factors that Lead to Conflict in the Context of the Post-2015 Agenda*, Saferworld, London.

Osinowo, A.A. (2015), *Combating Piracy in the Gulf of Guinea*, Africa Center for Strategic Studies, Washington, DC.

Ralston, L. (2014), *Trafficking and Fragility in West Africa*, World Bank, Washington, DC.

UN Comtrade (2015), *UN comtrade* (database), https://comtrade.un.org/db/default.aspx (accessed 1 September 2015).

UNODC (2014), *The Globalization of Crime: A Transnational Organized Crime Threat Assessment*, United Nations Office on Drugs and Crime, Vienna.

UNODC (2013), *Transnational Organized Crime in West Africa: A Threat Assessment*, United Nations Office on Drugs and Crime, Vienna.

UNODC (2011), *Estimating Illicit Flows from Drug Trafficking and other forms of Transnational Organized Crime*, United Nations Office on Drugs and Crime, Vienna.

UNODC (2009), *Transnational Trafficking and the Rule of Law in West Africa: A Threat Assessment*, United Nations Office on Drugs and Crime, Vienna.

UNSC (2013), "Letter dated 19 November 2013 from the Chair of the Security Council Committee established pursuant to Resolution 1521 (2003) concerning Liberia, addressed to the President of the Security Council (S/2013/683)", United Nations Security Council, New York.

ORGANISATION FOR ECONOMIC CO-OPERATION AND DEVELOPMENT

The OECD is a unique forum where governments work together to address the economic, social and environmental challenges of globalisation. The OECD is also at the forefront of efforts to understand and to help governments respond to new developments and concerns, such as corporate governance, the information economy and the challenges of an ageing population. The Organisation provides a setting where governments can compare policy experiences, seek answers to common problems, identify good practice and work to co-ordinate domestic and international policies.

The OECD member countries are: Australia, Austria, Belgium, Canada, Chile, the Czech Republic, Denmark, Estonia, Finland, France, Germany, Greece, Hungary, Iceland, Ireland, Israel, Italy, Japan, Korea, Latvia, Luxembourg, Mexico, the Netherlands, New Zealand, Norway, Poland, Portugal, the Slovak Republic, Slovenia, Spain, Sweden, Switzerland, Turkey, the United Kingdom and the United States. The European Union takes part in the work of the OECD.

OECD Publishing disseminates widely the results of the Organisation's statistics gathering and research on economic, social and environmental issues, as well as the conventions, guidelines and standards agreed by its members.

OECD PUBLISHING, 2, rue André-Pascal, 75775 PARIS CEDEX 16
(43 2015 08 1 P) ISBN 978-92-64-24520-4 – 2018

www.ingramcontent.com/pod-product-compliance
Ingram Content Group UK Ltd.
Pitfield, Milton Keynes, MK11 3LW, UK
UKHW051505290926
15471UKWH00008B/1427

9 789264 245204